TIMELESS INTERIORS

TIMELESS INTERIORS

ROOMS INSPIRED BY THE PAST

BARBARA STOELTIE   PHOTOGRAPHS BY RENÉ STOELTIE

FRANCES LINCOLN

Frances Lincoln Ltd
4 Torriano Mews
Torriano Avenue
London NW5 2RZ
www.franceslincoln.com

British Library Cataloguing-in-Publication data
A catalogue record for this book is available from the British Library.

ISBN 10: 0-7112-2610-5
ISBN 13: 978-0-7112-2610-4

Set in Caslon by Frances Lincoln Ltd

Printed in Singapore

9 8 7 6 5 4 3 2 1

PAGE 1 *Lars Sjöberg has assembled a
'Gustavian' still life of a Louis XV candlestick,
a pile of books and a reproduction eighteenth-
century drinking glass.*

PAGES 2-3 *Where once a seventies interior
made of formica, plastic and mirrored wall reigned
supreme, Frédéric Méchiche created an Adamesque
room with elegant Neoclassical features.*

THIS PAGE *In John Saladino's country retreat in
Connecticut, a collection of antique blue-and-white
plates grace the walls of one of the dining rooms.*

Contents

A TASTE FOR THE PAST 6

HOUSES TO REMEMBER 14

FIRST IMPRESSIONS 50

DRAWING ROOMS 62

DINING ROOMS 80

KITCHENS 94

LIBRARIES AND STUDIES 108

BEDROOMS 118

BATHROOMS 136

GARDEN ROOMS 148

SOURCE LIST 160

BIBLIOGRAPHY 165

INDEX 166

ACKNOWLEDGMENTS 168

A TASTE FOR THE PAST

'I was always searching for beauty. I wasn't as interested in the houses as I was in their ambience. In the furniture, in the history, in the garden. You never could put your finger specifically on whatever created the beauty, it was too elusive, but houses were where I found it the most . . .'

NANCY LANCASTER

NANCY LANCASTER'S WORDS echo my own feeling for interiors, which has been present from childhood. I grew up in Flanders – just after the Second World War – in the house of my great-grandmother. She lived in Ghent, in an eighteenth-century coachman's house at the back of a rather grand *hôtel particulier* in the purest Louis XV style. The memory of its interior details is so vivid that I do not need a Proustian tea-and-madeleine experience to go back in time and recall the checked black-and-white marble floor in the hall, the rounded shallow niche in the olive-green corridor where a robust brass tap provided fresh water, the labyrinth of tiny rooms and the massive cast-iron stoves.

My great-grandmother did not care for interior decoration. Like those animals who prefer to live in the discarded houses of other species, she installed herself among the embellishments left by previous occupants and she seemed in perfect harmony with her borrowed surroundings. Living with this formidable character who had one foot in the nineteenth century and the other – reluctantly – in the next was an unforgettable experience. My childhood world was made up almost entirely of anachronisms. At home, listening to music meant hearing the ancient operatic recordings of Caruso, Beniamino Gigli, Chaliapine and Nelly Melba (after whom the delicious peach melba ice at Grand-Mère's favourite local tea-room was named) on the wind-up gramophone. Reading meant choosing from titles such as *Uncle Tom's Cabin* or *Little Lord Fauntleroy*. The most exciting moments of the day were the visits of the milkman with his dog-cart, of the baker's errand-boy on his tricycle and – once a year – of the coal man with his rickety trailer and even more rickety Brabançon horse.

Quite unaware of the fact that I was living mainly in the past, I was absorbing all these images with the customary innocence of my tender age. And without acknowledging the peculiarity of the situation, I was rapidly developing a keen eye for 'period' details and 'period' living. Of course, the advent of 'modern times' could not be stopped, and in the early fifties I remember one of my aunts bursting with great excitement into our undamaged time-warp, carrying a load of wallpaper in her arms and shouting at the top of her voice that this particular kind of pattern – appropriately named 'Picasso' – was going to change our lives. But she met with the ice-cold stare of Grand-Mère and her refusal to let these barbaric, geometric designs besmirch our lovely home.

Other families were less conservative, and much later I learned that the revolutionary Scandinavian boomerang shapes had descended *en masse* upon the abodes of the more progressive members of the population. The fifties era had set in, but at home we were still clinging to Victorian values, Dickens and Puccini, while everyone else (so it seemed) was worshipping the new gods named Elvis and Rock and had been lured by pale Danish furniture, delicate paper Noguchi lamps and Aunt Renée's wretched Picasso wallpaper. The new household names were unpronounceable Scandinavian ones – Poul Kjaerholm, Finn Juhl and Alvar Aalto.

LEFT I have always found the urge to recreate the past irresistible. In my home in Holland, I have attempted to conjure up the restrained elegance of an eighteenth-century northern European grand salon.

The sixties heralded a most difficult period for me, for my adolescence was marked by a great struggle between my love for Grand-Mère's romantic world and my growing interest in all things 'modern'. Out went the sweet remembrance of the old coachman's house with its exquisite, old-fashioned rooms and in came the exciting iconoclasm of the Beatles, Mary Quant, the provocative mini-skirt and false eyelashes by the yard. Plastic reigned supreme, and inflatable, transparent furniture and chairs, lamps and kitchen utensils in screaming, vile colours took over from the natural Scandinavian look. Eileen Gray, Le Corbusier and their much-favoured combination of steel, chrome and black leather had yet to be rediscovered. For the moment the design-conscious sat decorously in Verner Panton's 'Champagne Chair' and in Knoll's pristine white and curvilinear furniture, or tried to look very futuristic and '2001' in a foam and stretch-jersey construction made by Monsieur Mourge.

More futuristic Vasarely patterns, the revolting combination of chocolate brown and orange and the dangerous juxtaposition of apple-green and geranium-red proved that the seventies were all about colour. And about colour-blindness. Walls covered with panels of brushed steel, long-haired flokati carpet that looked like the curly fur of a wet sheep and anthropomorphic furniture ran riot. To be really 'in' meant having perspex all over the place: a perspex coffee table, perspex side tables, perspex obelisks (with uplighters cleverly hidden in their bases so they glowed mysteriously at night) and little perspex supports and mounds to add 'drama' to the *objets d'art* and 'emphasize' (a word used profusely in American magazines during the seventies) their quality and value.

If interior design in the eighties had a colour scheme, it was mainly black and white. It was launched (and cleverly promoted) by the Black Widow of design, Andrée Putman, a gifted talent-scout and orchestrator

RIGHT In the basement kitchen of the Château de la Ferté Saint-Aubin, Jacques and Catherine Guyot have evoked the ambience of a bygone era by introducing period kitchen furniture and utensils.

of striking and severe interiors, who founded the firm ECART which reproduced original designs, mainly from the thirties. As a result, a large number of tables, chairs and lamps by the totally forgotten Irish designer Eileen Gray and creations by giants of the Art Deco period such as Robert Mallet-Stevens and Jean-Michel Frank were 're-edited'. Re-edition was the clever description that covered up the eighties' frantic and boundless copying of originals. Design fanatics, who would never have invested any money in the acquisition of a common copy, seemed to be proud to be living with the same Fortuny lamp, the same Eileen Gray carpet and the same sleek Frank sofa as their neighbours.

Those who thought that living amongst vulgar copies showed little originality seemed to find solace in the sublime and very aesthetic emptiness of minimalism, reassured by the fact that if one possessed very little one could never be accused of having no taste. Andrée Putman – always light years ahead of trends to come – had already pointed a warning finger at the threatening despotism of design and at 'the constant fear of not being of the latest fashion'. Frustration at not possessing the latest kettle, the hottest toothbrush or the last chair to sprout from the brilliant design spitting brain of Philippe Starck, led to a search for originality or to total despair.

Of course, the multi-faceted world of interior design had also had a string of adepts who would only take inspiration from great classical examples. In the fifties, when the boomerang fever had risen to its most dangerous level, the prominent French *décorateurs* Gérard Mille and Madeleine Castaing – to name but two – were filling the pages of the leading magazine *Connaissance des Arts* with images of rooms that looked deceptively 'period'. But Mille's love of white and gold and his penchant for velvets and damask silks and a flamboyant use of antiques seemed, at that time, only accessible to the moneyed few. Madame Castaing's subtle concoction

on eighteenth-century painting techniques, trompe l'oeil and the restoration of historical buildings, but also had an exceptional eye for colour. He amused his colleagues and clients with the bizarre names he gave to the paints he concocted from coarsely ground pigments following eighteenth-century practices. *'Vomitesse de la Reine'*, 'Elephant's Breath' and the scatological *'Caca du Dauphin'* now have a permanent place in the vocabulary of interior design. Fowler's rooms were masterpieces, and his employer and associate, the legendary Nancy Lancaster, with whom he ran the equally legendary London-based firm of Colefax and Fowler in Brook Street, described

of *le style Anglais*, bourgeois Viennese Biedermeier, and severe French Directoire reached its zenith at her own chateau near Chartres. But her cleverly composed 'windows on the past' were like wines that do not travel, and remained imprisoned in their own country.

In England, the gifted *connoisseur par excellence*, John Fowler, had spent more than three decades creating his highly personal vision of the English eighteenth-century room. Fowler (who believed himself to be the reincarnation of Marie-Antoinette, and who went through doors sideways to accommodate the imaginary *panier* under the Queen's dress) was not only an expert

him as someone who 'understood beautiful things and was drawn to them like a moth to a flame'.

This description could equally well apply to the formidable Mrs Lancaster herself, whose memories from her Virginia childhood transcribed in her splendid dwellings in England became the 'English country' look. Her 'buttah-yellah' room above the shop was seen as the epitome of relaxed chic, and some of her statements such as 'I never thought twice about using bright colours in old houses,' and 'Mahogany is lovely when it's been faded in the sun,' illustrate her loose interpretation of the past when she was attempting to create a 'period' look.

RIGHT *In the living room of his farmhouse, Dutch painter Cornelis le Mair has recklessly combined a few pieces of antique furniture, exotic fabrics, colourful china and home-made copies of seventeenth-century instruments.*

On the other side of the Atlantic, an equally formidable lady was also freely borrowing elements from the past. Lady Mendl – alias Elsie de Wolfe – who had actually invented the profession of 'interior decorator' was making a very risky cocktail of Louis styles in different shades of white and combining them with Venetian Baroque, forties' stucco, engraved mirrors and walls decorated with silver leaf.

Edith Wharton and Ogden Codman, who could not accept anything but 'powdered' Louis XVI and Directoire striped fabric, would have raised an eyebrow at the sight of Elsie's decorative acrobatics. Their purist approach to rooms usually meant turning them into perfect visions of eighteenth-century French *salons*. Their interiors created with elements from the past always gave the optical illusion of living in the past. Syrie Maugham's subtle 'pickling' and bleaching of her Georgian furniture, and the creative juggling of antiques and *objets d'art* practised by Rose Cummings, Ruby Ross Wood, Billy Baldwin, Sister Parish and Dorothy Draper, would never have met with approval from Wharton and her alter ego, because they were not authentic. But they were motivated by a genuine desire to use the past creatively. As Sister Parish once said in an interview, 'Innovation is often the ability to reach into the past and bring back what is beautiful, what is good, what is useful, what is lasting.'

In the late eighties, a photographic 'hunt' in London led us to Spitalfields, to the house of Dennis Severs, an American who had bought an eighteenth-century silk-weaver's house, which he had turned into an incredible 'period' illusion. We were told of rooms that looked as though they had not been touched since the time of the Georges – cobwebs and dust included – which were probably more evocative of the everyday life in the eighteenth century than Blenheim or Versailles. When we arrived in the sombre street, the sight of the tall, dark house with blood-red shutters provoked shivers of

Even the kitsch soundtrack that was supposed to conjure up the wheels of a carriage and the voices of Mrs Jarvis and her servants could not disturb the feeling that H.G. Wells' time-machine had become a reality.

Apart from the unique Severs experience, it is difficult to say exactly when we became aware of the growing interest in interiors that took their inspiration from the past. We are not talking of the fashionable accumulation of antiques, the incidental Georgian candlestick on the table or the fan that rests decoratively on a Louis XVI bergère

delight. What would we find inside? And what was the meaning of the straw on the pavement and the canary in the cage that hung from one of the shutters like some still life by Dutch master Carel Fabritius?

We were flabbergasted by Severs' labyrinth of Hogarthian candlelit rooms and by the delightfully mad way in which he had filled them with exactly the right canopied bed, bulky Georgian armchairs and even the correct chamber pot. Severs wanted his time-warp to provide 'something for the eye, something for the ear and something for the nose', and he had gone to enormous lengths to lead the visitor back to the period when the Jarvis family, well-to-do Huguenots, occupied the house.

in the boudoir, but of the all-consuming passion that leads decorators and non-decorators to do anything that will evoke the past in the tiniest detail. The fact is that suddenly it was there. Was it a rebellion against minimalism and a world invaded by technology and mass production? A form of escapism? Or nostalgia?

Whatever the reason, the desire for the patina of a bygone era is very powerful. Frédéric Méchiche, one of France's most prominent designers, has busied himself in his old fisherman's house in the south of France in an attempt to 'deceive the eye', furiously attacking his walls with a hammer and having them re-stuccoed as many times as necessary to achieve an age-worn surface.

Méchiche has proved over the years that he is a master of the most complicated means of achieving an illusion of age. He has stained his walls with pigment, milk and coffee, ground away at the edges of a stone staircase to create the impression of wear and tear, and applied layers of paint to a wall, only to scrape them off later to obtain a multi-layered look that could have been caused by centuries of repainting.

He is not alone in his efforts to evoke the past. French decorator Jacques Garcia has the genius to turn ruins into castles and castles into sophisticated ruins, and his 'period' rooms have attained such a degree of perfection that one would take an oath on their authenticity. Jacques and Catherine Guyot have struggled with the impressive empty shell of their Château de la Ferté Saint-Aubin, and gradually filled it with antique furniture, period portraits, canopied beds and even the appropriate copper pots, pans and kitchen utensils.

The setting for a 'period' recreation does not always have to be grand or the expenditure exorbitant. It is imagination rather than money that is the first requirement for originality. As Jean Cocteau once wrote, *'C'est l'empêchement qui fait créer'* (The struggle against opposition creates invention). Large amounts of money are not always needed: a room can be assembled from inexpensive finds in the flea market, a pair of old curtains and a table found in a street or on a skip. Ancient patinas have their own romance: crumbling walls and peeling paint can be the epitome of sophistication and touches such as the elegant folds of draped fabric, a candlestick

on an antique table or the presence of a canopied bed all contribute to a style that has been inspired by the past but will, in the end, be timeless.

The people whose work is featured in this book almost always have a penchant for accumulation and a feeling for history, poetry and theatre. This is the *leitmotiv* in the aesthetic vision of Dutch antiques dealer Ute Middelhoek, who carefully composes still lifes with blue-and-white china and with anything else from old tea towels to a yard of antique checked fabric and a basket of apples. It is the drive behind the bizarre collections in the home of her fellow-countryman, painter Cornelis le Mair, and in Lars Sjöberg's mania for collecting eighteenth-century Swedish country manors and exquisite Gustavian furniture for their interiors.

This book is full of rooms to remember – rooms that read like the pages of a storybook. And that they are nothing less than a tribute to the masters of illusion will come as no surprise. We hope they will show that nothing is more fascinating than to draw upon the past, to please the eye and to bewilder and enchant. As the French writer, poet and *femme d'esprit* Louise de Vilmorin once wrote:

> *'Nos maisons sont nos prisons*
> *Sachons y retrouver la liberté*
> *Dans la façon de les parer.'*

> 'Our homes are our prisons
> let us try to regain our freedom
> in the way we decorate them.'

HOUSES TO REMEMBER

A DUTCH
MANOR

I T ALL BEGAN with an advertisement in the newspaper: 'Apartment to let in seventeenth-century castle.' Being insatiably curious we visited it right away, and that was our big mistake. Can anyone resist the charms of a sleepy Dutch village, its Gothic church surrounded by meadows and orchards and, down a drive, hidden by trees, a manor house encircled by moats that could have been lifted straight from a Dutch Old Master?

We hardly listened to the agent's guided tour. We were too busy lapping up the Louis XV panelling, the tall

PREVIOUS PAGES *The house in winter.*
LEFT *In the living room the Louis XV panelling was painted a Georgian green and all the carvings picked out in off-white. An eighteenth-century French* lit de repos *sits in front of the tall window, and the French Directoire table is surrounded by late eighteenth-century Italian chairs.*
ABOVE *On the grey marble mantel a Sèvres 'biscuit' bust on a plinth, engravings, a book and a delicate porcelain cup echo the eighteenth-century taste for artfully arranged 'clutter'.*

ABOVE *In the bathroom, a Neoclassical plaster bust on a plinth,*
a cast-iron tripod, and a Louis XVI ormolu candlestick have been
juxtaposed with a modern stone sphinx and wooden obelisk to
create an elegant ensemble.

OPPOSITE *On the kitchen wall there is an early nineteenth-*
century comtoise *clock without its case. The Louis XV sofa was*
upholstered in a blue-and-white checked cotton to emphasize the
distinctly 'northern' feel of the room and to complement the blue
washed walls and eighteenth-century English tilt-top table.
A great deal of attention has been given to the arrangement of
copper pots and pans and antique kitchen utensils; there is even a
clever modern copy of an eighteenth-century sugar loaf.

windows with their staggering views, the parquet floor, the grey marble fireplace and the austere bathroom with its central tub. It suddenly dawned on us how delightful it would be to conjure up rooms that looked as if nothing had been altered for centuries: a time-warp, an illusion, a three-dimensional trompe l'oeil.

It was time to roll up our sleeves. A plaster bust from the *atelier* of Houdon, a Swedish Gustavian bracket clock and a bed draped *à la Polonaise* were the only props necessary to play a wicked visual trick on the casual observer.

We have picked up inspiration and furniture on our travels, from sources that have often been forgotten. Today, we sometimes ask ourselves where we unearthed that typical Georgian green we used to daub the eighteenth-century panelling in the drawing room. The idea for the colour of our kitchen – a washed blue that was famous throughout the eighteenth century for being fly repellent – may have come from Jacques Garcia's Château Menou or from memories of a visit to a period Dutch farmhouse – we can't be too sure. And after all, what does it matter?

Have we succeeded in recreating an eighteenth-century look? Some friends have warned us that we will soon be wearing powdered wigs and period costumes. When we contemplate our kitchen with its ancient pans and utensils, our bathroom that looks as though Pauline Bonaparte might step in at any moment and the romantic glow of candlelight that fills our apartment each evening, we have to admit they have a point.

A PROVENÇAL HIDING PLACE

 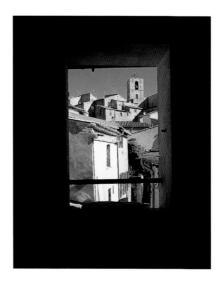 

THE PLASTERERS putting the final delicate touches to their work – remodelling the windowsills in the sitting room of a tiny Provençal fisherman's house – witnessed the arrival of its owner with apprehension. Frédéric Méchiche came armed with a hammer and a wicked-looking wire brush. Then the first blows fell and the artisans watched aghast as their beautiful, skimmed finish succumbed to a hail of whacks and gouges.

This now celebrated incident crowned an interesting new phase in the career of the famous French decorator, a man who for years had been celebrated for his perfectly tailored interiors. He was also in the habit of saying that he despised the Côte d'Azur. A few years ago, however, he managed to overcome his horror of the French Riviera for long enough to visit a friend in the area who claimed to have found a haven of peace. Strolling through the narrow, twisting streets of an ancient town with a Romanesque church, he was suddenly confronted with 'a small, tall house, eaten away by time, unusually beautiful and up for sale.'

The estate agent's description of 'warped' floors and 'appalling' condition were enough to whet his appetite. Méchiche was on the lookout for things authentic and deeply suspicious of terms like 'luxury', 'fully restored' and 'impeccable', saying 'I'd rather contemplate a door and a few windows with their paint peeling off!'

Where the patina of centuries did not exist, Frédéric Méchiche invented it. First of all, he astonished the whole neighbourhood by climbing up a ladder and plastering

LEFT In the drawing room, pale lavender walls form a perfect backdrop for Directoire furniture, and a Provençal corner cupboard and terracotta water cistern, both painted off-white.

ABOVE An eighteenth-century cupboard near the staircase hides a secret refrigerator. From one of the tiny windows there is a splendid view over neighbouring houses and the medieval church. In the master bedroom a Provençal table, a Louis XV chair covered in toile de Jouy, a drawing, a frosted glass candlestick, an antique bottle, and some flowers and foliage in a glass make a still life that could have been painted by Chardin.

LEFT In a corner of the living room is a French Louis XV chair with its original silk damask upholstery. Shells, a few pieces of white coral, a Directoire tin wall light, an eighteenth-century painting and a cardboard box decorated with period wallpaper all contribute to the deceptively 'period' ambience.

RIGHT In a tiny bedroom the window has been draped with antique linen. A Directoire chair with white cotton upholstery, a white antique Provençal cotton bedspread, a creamy rug from Cogolin, white woodwork and a crystal chandelier convey an impression of crispness.

OVERLEAF LEFT The peeling green paint on the walls of the staircase displays Méchiche's mastery of distressed effects. The stone stairs reinforced with wood are original.

OVERLEAF RIGHT The stucco walls of the guest bedroom have been deliberately 'distressed', while the ceiling beams have been left undisturbed. A Louis XVI chair upholstered in plain white linen (actually a coarsely woven antique sheet), an eighteenth-century Provençal writing table holding a Directoire lamp and a simple Louis XVI mirror with a worn glass contribute to the room's visual calm.

the entire surface of his façade with an ochre paste, daubing it with evil-smelling mud and drenching the result with hundreds of litres of greasy, opaque water to recreate the effect of age. Then a team of masons, carpenters and painters came and went for six months, and Méchiche spent weeks going round the demolition yards of the region, tracking down eighteenth-century architectural salvage.

The house was furnished with pieces found locally or in the capital. From the Toulon flea market came a fine armoire, which was immediately painted a dark Provençal green. Paris yielded eighteenth-century chairs and some 'crushed strawberry' toile de Jouy. At the Le Lavandou flea market Méchiche unearthed china, old linen and the ancient terracotta pots that adorn the tiny roof terrace.

The sober eighteenth-century pieces, unusual garden furniture, worn mirrors and tin light fixtures are perfectly offset by the deliberately mutilated, stained and faded walls, painted in the tones of an old watercolour. The only modern piece of furniture in the house, a large, deep and comfortable sofa, is simply covered with a slipcover made from nineteenth-century linen bedsheets. Whenever he feels threatened by perfection, Méchiche's response is vigorous. Even now he can sometimes be heard exclaiming that some door frame or chair arm 'needs a touch of age'. And when his eye catches a slightly too smooth piece of paintwork above the sofa, the hammer and the wire brush are ready to hand.

A NEW ENGLAND HOME

W HEN SHARON AND JEFFREY CASDIN discovered an eighteenth-century clapboard house in the heart of Berkshire County, Massachusetts, they were immediately taken with the unadorned and somewhat severe classical façade, the grand front door and the neat rows of period sash windows. Once inside, they realized that this miraculously preserved relic of the colonial era, with its original paintwork, undisturbed architectural features and beautifully distressed walls, would demand an unconditionally purist approach to decoration.

Blessed with generous proportions, high ceilings, ornate mouldings and an imposing entrance hall, the house was not exactly a cosy weekend hideaway for a New York-based family. Nevertheless, Sharon, Jeffrey and their children decided to move in and spend some time amidst the crumbling walls with their centuries-old patina, before making any attempt to decorate or embellish. They realized they had acquired a valuable window on the past – 'a fly in amber' – and they wanted to preserve its weathered beauty.

Advice was sought from their decorator, close friend and not-too-distant neighbour, John Saladino, who agreed with the Casdins' almost 'archaeological' approach. This involved painstakingly peeling off layers of wallpaper, gently scraping away the too recent paint and – where necessary – delicately sponging the walls with natural pigments to echo the original colour of a room.

The final result was a set of rooms of museum quality. Chalky white walls in the drawing room, a warm cinnamon hue in one of the guest rooms and battered greyish-green panelling in the entrance hall now serve as a perfect backdrop for a set of slip-covered Georgian chairs, a fine selection of Shaker furniture (antique and reproduction) and an array of well-chosen decorative objects and Indian artefacts.

ABOVE Built more than two centuries ago for a Boston settler, the clapboard house still has its original sash windows and classical front door.

LEFT The entrance hall has wide floorboards and period panelling. Layers of modern paint were scraped off to reveal the original eighteenth-century colour underneath. Furnishings are restricted to a Shaker chair and a wooden chest, in keeping with the spare style of eighteenth-century decorating.

OVERLEAF In the drawing room (left), walls were stripped of layers of wallpaper to reveal chalky white stucco. The Georgian chairs are covered in plain white cotton and on the mantel is a display of dried flowers, a creamware tureen and an Indian headdress. The reflector wall lamps are reproductions of eighteenth-century originals. The guest room (right) can be glimpsed beyond the drawing room. An antique wooden birdcage by the shutter completes this vision of Vermeer-like tranquillity.

The hearth in the guest bedroom (opposite) is original to the house. John Saladino advised on the colour and suggested using a traditional 'sponging' technique to apply natural pigments to the walls. The cast-iron candlestick and the Shaker chair are faithful reproductions of originals. Although the twin four-posters (this page) are reproductions of original Shaker beds, the choice of fabrics, old-fashioned coverlets and the superb patina on the walls lend an aura of authenticity.

AFTER THE OLD MASTERS

THE DUTCH artist Cornelis le Mair (known to his friends as Cees) is one of the most controversial painters in the Low Countries. After a bohemian existence in his native town of Eindhoven and years of apprenticeship at the Academy of Fine Arts in Antwerp, he returned to Eindhoven in the mid 1970s, where he found a derelict old farmhouse.

Le Mair's appearance is as unsettling and anachronistic as his art. With his long hair, Rembrandtesque moustache and goatee, eighteenth-century jacket and matching *chemise*, he seems out of sympathy with our computerized age. His oil paintings of Pre-Raphaelite beauties smothered in crushed velvets and roses (or wearing nothing at all), and his still lifes which are said to be the technical equal of those by the seventeenth-century Dutch masters, have won him both admiration and criticism. His is an eccentric world, and it comes as no surprise that he has decorated his home with an eclectic mix of dried flowers, feathers, sequinned or embroidered oriental fabrics and Delft tiles.

For some people a visit to the house might result in a serious attack of visual indigestion. The accumulation of objects and furniture, the dangerous juxtaposition of elements such as a heavily carved column from Rajasthan, a reclining bed covered with layers of Indian fabrics, stained-glass windows and a *vanitas* composition complete with yellowing human skulls, creates an atmosphere that bears no resemblance to the modern image of the artist's studio. Instead, the combination of oriental splendours and kitsch – masses of macramé lamps and flimsy, glittering veils – gives his home a seventeenth-century ambience. There is panelling painted with seventeenth-century-style landscapes, paintings that suggest the hand of an Old Master and musical instruments that le Mair has made himself.

When evening comes, the era of Rembrandt and his followers becomes even more tangible as le Mair lights the lamps and myriad objects glow mysteriously in the dark. There is nothing to remind one of the twentieth century outside.

ABOVE Although the gazebo at the back of the garden looks like a relic from the past, le Mair built it himself only a few decades ago from salvaged materials. It is now used for afternoon tea, and the roof houses his colony of doves.
RIGHT Le Mair's special way with pattern is evident in the living room. The daring assembly of geometric tiles, hand-painted Delft, colourful tapestry, heavily decorated Victorian furniture, Indian macramé, lamps and fabrics could easily have resulted in a hideously ugly interior, but le Mair gets away with murder.

LEFT *In a corner of the living room, le Mair has installed a sumptuous day bed made from an ornately sculpted column he found in Rajasthan and a sofa draped with oriental fabrics. On display are some of the musical instruments he has made: mandolins, hurdy-gurdies and guitars. The stained-glass windows are original to the house.*

OVERLEAF LEFT *In the bedroom, le Mair has draped the bed (his own creation) with diaphanous, sequinned silk saris brought back from India. The oriental patchwork throw hides a painted Victorian table, and a nineteenth-century rustic chair has also been covered with a similar patchwork. Rugs – good and bad – cover the floor.*

OVERLEAF RIGHT *The bathroom (top right) has the same atmosphere of* haute bohême. *An embroidered canopy – originally part of an Indian tent – hangs over the washbasin. The oil lamp is made of opal glass and the earthenware pitcher is a nineteenth-century copy of a vessel seen in seventeenth-century still lifes.*

All the painting in the house was done by the artist himself, and in his tiny kitchen (bottom right) he has covered the panels of the units with flowers. Old-fashioned tea towels, Indian banners and old kitchen utensils hang from the beams, and shelves are laden with old kitchenware, tins and jars. In the middle of the hearth is a cast-iron Dutch pot-bellied stove.

In the anteroom leading to one of le Mair's studios (top left and bottom left), Indian fabrics and embroidered panels run riot. The ceiling and walls have been almost entirely covered with antique exotic fabrics. Under the dormer window a late-nineteenth-century organ awaits le Mair's flamboyant decoration.

A SUFFOLK BARN

IN THE MID 1980S, London antiques dealer Keith Skeel went to Suffolk to visit friends and fell in love with the countryside there. It took him only a few months to lay his hands on a mid-nineteenth-century house on a hill in Peasonhall, near Saxmundham: a square construction with long windows on the ground floor and a cast-iron balcony strangely reminiscent of a plantation mansion in nineteenth-century Louisiana. He decorated it in the flamboyant style, with many Victorian touches, that has become his trademark.

Behind the house there was a large barn – an empty shell that had served as a shelter for generations of owls. Skeel immediately saw its potential for conversion into a guest house, realizing that it would give him the opportunity to show his skill at recreating a rustic, more subdued country style.

First, however, he had to replan the interior of the barn. On the ground floor enough room was created for a romantic, old-fashioned kitchen, complete with worn sink, pine shelving and a winding, stone staircase. The former hayloft on the first floor, with its intricate geometrical pattern of ancient beams, was converted into one large unpartitioned space to serve as both sitting room and bedroom. The walls were carefully restored and whitewashed, and a special finish was applied to give them a timeworn look.

To furnish the barn, Skeel was able to take his pick from the brass kettles, pestle and mortars, antique quilts and painted corner cupboards in his shops. Today an array of simple chairs and benches, whose plain lines create a strong graphic framework, alternate with gleaming brass objects, an antique brass and mahogany bed, romantic needlework, faded rugs and a vast collection of pewter jugs and plates. The overall effect is that of a well-kept gentleman farmer's retreat, where life unfolds serenely, disturbed only by the ticking of the clock .

A CONNECTICUT RETREAT

WHEN INTERIOR DESIGNER John Saladino and his late wife Virginia discovered this stone house in north-west Connecticut, they were smitten with the beauty of its architecture. Although it was clear from the start that it required major restoration and decoration, they did not hesitate to buy it. Robin Hill, apparently named after the multitude of robins that populate the grounds, was built in the 1920s, combining Great Gatsby-style luxury with Georgian revival taste. John Saladino perfected and refined its architecture, adding extra rooms and elements such as Georgian fanlights, a wonderful *oeil-de-boeuf* window and an early American spiral staircase saved from destruction in a far-away country house. Nowadays, Robin Hill, with its elongated front, central loggia and surrounding romantic garden with clipped topiary and architectural ornaments, appears to conjure up restrained, late-eighteenth-century elegance.

Saladino's knowledge of historical colours and traditional painting techniques, and his own amazing sense of colour, have resulted in a series of rooms with very personal schemes. There are stunning combinations such as 'greys-with-a-violet-tinge' with pale lavender, and muted rusty ochres with 'raspberry ice' and off-white. In the dining room, a Neoclassical fireplace, eighteenth-century silver and Italian creamware tureens, urns and plates have been successfully 'married' with a major work by modern artist Cy Twombly and slip-covered chairs. In the living room a spectacular Grinling Gibbons fireplace and a pair of bookcases attributed to Chippendale sit happily with comfortable and very twentieth-century seating and modern frescoes of gardens. Although Saladino has looked to both Georgian England and Imperial Rome for inspiration, his home is not a dictatorial period reconstruction without contemporary comforts.

ABOVE The house was built in the 1920s, but Saladino's embellishments have given it an eighteenth-century feel.
RIGHT In the 'den', antique pine panelling rescued from another house and mauve walls provide a backdrop for
American country furniture, a rare Irish chair and modern necessities such as the television and telephones.

LEFT *Saladino is a master at mixing periods and styles while keeping an overall effect of homogeneity. The decorative scheme in Robin Hill's generously proportioned drawing room is a perfect illustration of one of his mottoes: 'Everything is in the colour.' He has combined faded antique rugs, a pair of spectacular Chippendale bookcases, sturdy slip-covered Colonial armchairs, Louis XVI* corbeille *chairs, a breathtaking early nineteenth-century grisaille wallpaper screen and fabrics such as antique velvet, faded silks and plain cottons.*

OVERLEAF LEFT *In the dining room pale lavender walls and an Adamesque fireplace set off the subtle display of John and Virginia's exquisite collection of raspberry-coloured lustre-ware and a spectacular eighteenth-century creamware lidded vase.*

OVERLEAF RIGHT *Saladino designed the rounded, slip-covered chairs in the summer dining room and combined them, despite their obviously contemporary shape, with an eighteenth-century wooden table, period candlesticks, a striking Neoclassical blue vase, antique porcelain plates and an exceptional eighteenth-century blue glass Indian lantern. The vaulted ceiling decorated with a cloud pattern emphasizes the Italianate character of the room.*

47

FIRST
IMPRESSIONS

THE ENTRANCE HALL AND STAIRCASE are the introduction to a house, and architects and decorators have tried over the centuries to turn it into their *pièce de resistance.* After all, it is only human to judge our neighbours' taste (or lack of it) the moment we set foot in their homes. We mentally prepare ourselves for the splendours and the horrors to come, while letting our eyes wander around the entrance hall, casting a critical glance at the floor, the longcase clock in the corner, the curve of the balustrade or the colour of the walls.

What a pity that there is no record of Louis XIV's reaction when first he entered Fouquet's palatial hall in the Château of Vaux-le-Vicomte in July 1660. Was he green with envy when he saw the huge dome and the rows of marble busts on the typical Louis XIV plinths, and did he make a scene? Or did he smile knowingly, having already made up his mind to send his cheeky Minister of Finances to the darkest cell of the Bastille?

During the Middle Ages, halls were grand and draughty, often equipped with a monumental fireplace where a roaring fire did its best to chase out the biting cold. But by the seventeenth century, floorboards, carved oak staircases and tapestries were adding more comfort and warmth to the Arctic atmosphere. Around this time, some halls developed into rooms where the owner's wealth could be tastefully displayed in a simplified version of the *kunstkammer* (art gallery), complete with intricately inlaid marble floors, statues on plinths or grand chandeliers.

This potent image may linger in the mind, inspiring grand visions of period entrance halls, but the reality of reproducing them is a different matter. We may dream of trying our hand at a reduced version of the long-defunct Escalier des Ambassadeurs at Versailles and juggle dangerously with bits of coloured marble. We might want to construct our own Sanssouci, throw in a few columns, cover our walls with the softest possible shade of grey and hang a delicate crystal chandelier from a ceiling that has been painted to resemble an overcast sky. But in the end we tend to succumb *en masse* to the simple charms of the Georgian entrance hall, its staircase with twisted balusters and a sturdy mahogany handrail, a modest skylight and the inevitable strip of carpet that so baffled the French traveller Rochefoucauld when he visited England in the 1780s, that he commented: 'You are upon mats and carpets everywhere and there is always a strip of drugget on the stairs.'

It is the entrance hall that introduces the 'colour' of our historical inspirations to our visitors. From here, we take them by the hand and wickedly test their reactions to visual tricks such as roughly plastered walls covered with natural pigment, an oak staircase bought from a salvage yard, a Swedish chair with a rush seat from an auction and a few eighteenth-century engravings from a market stall. Will our visitors express their admiration and congratulate us for having found such an unspoilt 'period' home? Or will they smell a rat and unmask the striped wallpaper in the niche by the door that has been stained with black tea to give it an aged look?

Nancy Lancaster – an inspired artist who spent her whole life doing up houses – has left a most delightful description of the decoration of the staircase in her London townhouse at 28 Queen Anne's Gate: 'When you walked in, the staircase was on the left: it was the loveliest architectural feature in the house. I left the staircase a tobacco colour but painted the panelling along the stairs a pale, pale green. On the window in the stair hall I put curtains the colour of a cigar, with a fringed pelmet and along the floor I had a very pretty Bessarabian runner with the same brown in it . . .' Her words convey something of the excitement involved in creating this prologue to the performance.

PREVIOUS PAGES In the entrance hall of Gary Tinterow's and James Joseph's Hudson Valley retreat, everything has been pared down to the minimum. Ancient floorboards and a refined but spartan staircase are given special prominence, and tribute is paid to the Colonial era in the subtle eighteenth-century colour scheme of putty-coloured walls and delicate green panelling. The red damask silk of the upholstery on the early American chair stands out dramatically against the pale background.

LEFT *When she designed the hall in this Jacobean manor house in Somerset, Phillipa Naess chose to emphasize the basic architectural elements – the slate-coloured worn flagstone floor and the dramatic fall of light in the interior – by furnishing it with just a few select pieces. A Jacobean table and a framed print by Henry Moore steal the show, while a period chair with cabriolet legs and a brass lantern complete this image of timeless beauty.*

RIGHT *Undeterred by the small scale of the entrance hall in his Parisian flat, antiques dealer Serge Hubert created an impact by using the kind of pieces normally seen in a larger space. An early nineteenth-century marble tazza stands on a scagliola column, flanked by two Neoclassical wrought-iron stools equipped with faux leopard cushions. A large square mirror, ormolu wall-sconces and a bell-shaped glass ceiling lamp complete a decorative scheme that pays homage to the austere Directoire style.*

PREVIOUS PAGES LEFT *In Anna and Günther Lambert's late eighteenth-century chateau, the severe elegance of the entrance hall with its tiled marble floor, imposing stairs and wrought-iron balustrade is softened by the ochre wash delicately sponged on the walls, and the warmth of the stripped wooden doors. A sea-grass runner provides comfort on the stairs, while wrought-iron armchairs, a table and a round mirror with a gilt frame add interest to the passageway.*

PREVIOUS PAGES RIGHT *Attention to detail is just as important in entrance halls as it is elsewhere in the house. In the hall leading to the conservatory of their Victorian house in the south of Holland, Dutch antiques dealers Karel and Will Leenaers have created a strong focal point by introducing a polychrome, late eighteenth-century Italian console table and hanging an earlier English portrait above it. An antique earthenware vessel, a pair of hurricane lamps and a few plants in terracotta pots make an enchanting still life that echoes the delicate colour scheme of the room.*

OPPOSITE *When he arived at this chateau in Normandy, Frédéric Méchiche was faced with four walls, a decaying floor and a missing roof. Everything – including the hall and staircase – had to be reassembled or 'faked'. 'Period' wooden stairs were installed, and artificially worn and hollowed by an industrial sanding machine. The stone floor with its black marble lozenges is also a recent addition. The only genuinely period element in the entrance hall is the Louis XVI barometer.*

LEFT ABOVE *French interior designer Didier Rabes successfully 'faked' the grand staircase of a French eighteenth-century chateau in a loft-like space (once part of the couture studio of Madeleine Vionnet) by introducing a flight of stairs with a wrought-iron balustrade and a traditional stone floor inlaid with black diamonds, and adding a mirror in imitation of an* oeil-de-boeuf *window. Rabes never hesitates to use architectural features made of stucco or even resin, because in his opinion everything that leads to an illusion of authenticity is justified.*

LEFT CENTRE *Bright orange-red covers the walls of this otherwise dark and gloomy entrance hall in a French country house. A nineteenth-century English hall chair, period stairs with a wrought-iron balustrade and an ancient hunting trophy form a strong contrast with the vibrant colour on the walls. The use of strong colours was common throughout the eighteenth century.*

LEFT BELOW *In the entrance hall of a charming French Directoire house, whitewashed walls and a dado that has been painted dark green form the ideal backdrop for a terracotta bust of Apollo Belvedere, and for the period staircase with its polished wooden stairs, handrail and gleaming copper finial.*

LEFT *Landings, halls and lobbies can become repositories of hidden treasures. Ute Middelhoek has turned her first floor landing into an extra room by decorating it with period furniture, framed antique textiles, and an array of eighteenth- and nineteenth-century earthenware and porcelain jugs, bowls and pots. This is also where she displays her collection of antique cardboard storage boxes and the French nineteenth-century painted papier-mâché heads that once served as supports for headdresses, hats or wigs.*

RIGHT *In a house in Massachusetts, a lobby leading off the wooden panelled hall has become a perfect storage place for the inevitable chaos of boots, wellingtons, sports equipment, coats and hats, all presided over by a framed study of George Washington.*

DRAWING
ROOMS

I AM AFRAID THE DRAWING ROOM would have seemed quite wrong to the editors of *Vogue* or *House and Garden*', wrote Julien Green in his *Memories of Happy Days* (1942). 'For one thing, the furniture was ill assorted and created an effect of confusion. There was an elephantine chesterfield under a gas chandelier, and by the door an upright piano of dark wood. Armchairs of various descriptions were arranged in a semicircle around the mantelpiece and seemed to be discussing the holes in the hearth-rug . . .'

Green's description of his parents' *débût-de-siècle* flat on the rue de Passy in Paris will send shivers down the spine of all who swear by the laws of Le Corbusier, or fill their drawing rooms with the latest designs. But for those who crave a romantic effect, the reading of these lines will be a sheer delight.

PREVIOUS PAGES LEFT *In this English Jacobean manor house, interior designer Philippa Naess has succeeded in creating a drawing room that complements the severe grandeur of the architecture. Dark-toned rich velvets, kilims, tapestry, oriental carpets with faded colours and the occasional antique, high-backed armchair create a warm and welcoming atmosphere in a room where light and sun are welcome as guests rather than intruders.*

PREVIOUS PAGES RIGHT *Colourful carpets, Colonial armchairs covered with white cotton covers, an eighteenth-century English-style sofa upholstered with a cheerful striped fabric, a large floral painting, cream walls, Venetian blinds and a tall English 'bureau-cabinet' have transformed this former landing in an early nineteenth-century house in the New Orleans French Quarter into a light and often sun-drenched drawing room. Cotton or linen covers are practical and inexpensive to make and always add a touch of freshness.*

If one were to buy a French chateau – let's say an impressive building dating from the time of Louis XIV – one could perfectly well try to ignore the panelling, the period fireplaces, the chestnut-coloured *parquet-de-Versailles* and the elaborate stucco ceilings. One could set a tornado of off-white matt paint racing through the house, furnish the drawing room with a few sofas, chairs and a lamp straight from a design catalogue, throw in a few pieces of contemporary art, and the effect would be both daring and stunning. If one wanted the room to look as if Madame de Maintenon could walk in at any moment, the proceedings would be different. And that is what this chapter is all about.

Of all the rooms in the house, the drawing room has been the one most affected by changing fashions through the centuries, for our drawing rooms are our visiting cards. We do not always let people into our bathrooms, we may be careful not to show the laboratory where our meals are prepared, and our bedrooms are often 'inner sanctums', so intimate and personal that we prefer to protect them from prying eyes.

But we are far less worried about exposing our drawing rooms to the critical gaze of strangers, even though our choice of colours, paintings, fabrics, ornaments, furniture and lighting gives away our deepest emotions and – worst of all – will result in our visitors' merciless verdict on our taste. Taste – which has kept historians, aesthetes and the whole creative world busy for thousands of years – is responsible for our moods in decoration and endless aesthetic suffering. Under its dictatorial pressure our drawing-room walls have been variously embellished with panelling carved with 'grotesques' during the Renaissance, Cordoban leather a century later, flock wallpaper and silk under the Georges and the Louises,

Neoclassical grisaille panels during the Empire and a reckless mixture of all these in the nineteenth century! Taste has also proclaimed that whereas one day we received our visitors in a carved high-back chair upholstered in velvet, the next day we would be seated in an overstuffed bergère covered in *soie de Lyon*.

Seventeenth-century tastemakers advised us to banish carpets from our living quarters because they were notorious for absorbing powder from wigs, but their nineteenth-century counterparts told us to have plenty of carpets and to keep away the unhealthy draughts that today we would rechristen 'fresh air'. And to make things worse, taste has pointed its despotic claw in the direction of our fireplaces, where we have graduated from burning logs in a hearth to burning coal beneath an elegant Adam mantelpiece, finally ripping out the entire grate and replacing it with a cast-iron stove.

If we believed the French saying *'Les goûts et les couleurs ne se discutent pas'* (One does not argue about taste and colour) we would really be lost to the dictates of fashion. We need freedom to mix styles and epochs and to let the imagination run wild. It is this sense of freedom, the conviction that one has the absolute right to turn a drawing room into a frivolous Parisian salon, a severe Georgian 'withdrawing-room' or a spartan Shaker-like parlour that has motivated those who have created the amazing drawing rooms in this chapter. Their boldness in treating their main reception room as a stage for illusion makes for tremendous visual excitement.

Imagination is the key to transforming a room's identity. In his novel *Roxana* (1724), Daniel Defoe describes his heroine's creative decorating tricks: 'I had a large dining room in my apartments, with five other rooms on the same floor, all of which I made drawing rooms for the occasion, having all the beds taken down for the day; in three of these I had tables plac'd, cover'd with wine and sweetmeats; the fourth had a green table for play, and the fifth was my own room where I sat, and where I receiv'd all the company that came to pay their compliments to me . . .' Roxana undoubtedly had inventiveness and style.

There is an aphorism: 'Taste is what you buy in the shops, style is how you put it together.' Having 'style' inspired by the past means leaving the dust and the patina of your eighteenth-century panelling undisturbed, turning all your attention to the furniture and, if necessary, travelling the world to find the wall sconces and the candlesticks that will provide that precise quality of light that you are looking for. Style means turning your drawing room into a Gothic folly, a Victorian hunting lodge, a cocotte's love-nest with masses of bows and frills or a cool Adamesque 'saloon' that would have been envied by Beau Brummel.

Those who have struggled to obtain the romantic portrait that goes so well with the floral chintz on the armchair, and who have faced the excitement and the disappointments of the auction room to lay their greedy hands on that pair of fire dogs without which the fireplace would never be complete, also know the frisson of possessing the past. They will surely feel a pang of recognition in these lines from Balzac's *Cousin Pons*: 'The last forty years the apartment had remained unaltered. The paint, the wallpaper, the furnishings, everything reminded one of the Empire style. Forty years of dust and smoke had tarnished the mirrors, the mouldings, the pattern of the paper, the ceilings and the paintwork . . .' Rarely have a few lines on a set of rooms expressed so aptly the atmosphere of an interior frozen in time.

OPPOSITE *When the owners of this Biedermeier town house moved in, the appearance of the drawing room was a far cry from its present splendours. Over a period of years, floorboards and doors were sanded and scrubbed, the surrounds were decorated with a deliberately clumsy faux-marble in imitation of the style of country decorators, walls were painted a bright Biedermeier blue, and the fireplace was transformed into a niche with a fat classical column and given a fresh coat of whitewash.*

THIS PAGE *In a New York apartment, interior designer John Saladino combined several rooms to obtain one grand drawing room with an elegant Neoclassical feel. Slender columns divide the space, the walls are a soft pale grey and a Louis XV giltwood console table provides a focal point at one end. A pair of clipped standard bay trees, Neoclassical chairs, stools and comfortable armchairs (designed by Saladino) have been arranged symmetrically to emphasize the strict classical order of this decorative scheme.*

LEFT *The right fireplace is a key element when one is trying to create the perfect 'period' room. In this drawing room in the northern Netherlands, the owners added a French sandstone Louis XVI fireplace of restrained design to match the austere olive-green antique wall panelling – also a new addition – and the original tall windows. They also installed the terracotta tiled floor and furnished the room with Biedermeier and Empire furniture and paintings. No one could possibly guess that this atmospheric drawing room was once a pub lounge with a formica and plastic interior.*

RIGHT *In an eighteenth-century former farmer's house, Anna and Günther Lambert have made a charming drawing room by installing Directoire panelling and adding a plain early nineteenth-century fireplace. A blend of new and old patinas, a carefully placed ancient wicker basket and an unframed copy of a Picasso still life that 'melts' into the panelling, combine to create an idyllic mood.*

LEFT *The owners of this Massachusetts house kept the whitewashed and roughly stuccoed walls and restored them delicately without disturbing the original patina. The same happened to the floorboards, the shutters and the panelling, and although most of the furniture is modern, the ambience of the drawing room is true to the eighteenth-century architecture.*

RIGHT ABOVE *Nothing has been altered in this striking room in an American country house. The only additions were an eighteenth-century mezzotint, a high-back Colonial chair, a pair of brass firedogs and a truly spectacular antique day-bed with its original horsehair upholstery. Horsehair upholstery is still being produced today, and it now comes in many colours and patterns besides the traditional plain black. The lack of carpets accentuates the room's spartan beauty.*

RIGHT BELOW *The owners of this apartment in a brand-new Swiss chalet (built with traditional materials and in a typical Swiss style) searched Switzerland and Germany to find the eighteenth-century pitch-pine panelling for their drawing room. Belgian decorator Benoît Vliegen introduced the painted armoire, the Louis XV side table, the contemporary and comfortable sofa, and the Lloyd Loom chair.*

LEFT *In a former artist's studio in an early twentieth-century Paris apartment building, Frédéric Méchiche conjured up an eighteenth-century ambience by introducing a set of Austrian portraits, a classical parquet floor of his own design, and a guéridon and candlestick that are perfectly in keeping with the period. The formal Louis XVI small sofa and armchairs have been upholstered not in the obvious damask silk, but in a striped cotton designed by Méchiche.*

RIGHT *The charming carved details on Rococo sofas provide the perfect complement for all kinds of upholstery. A Swedish Louis XV giltwood sofa (above) has been covered with a traditional Swedish blue-and-white cotton fabric. Although the result may look very modern, the use of checked cotton fabric or its equivalent in silk (for royal palaces and grand manor houses) was very popular during the Gustavian period.*

A mid-eighteenth-century Italian sofa (centre) is upholstered in black calfskin, which forms a striking contrast with the floral glazed chintz on the wall behind.

A nineteenth-century Italian pseudo-Louis XV sofa with a black and gold frame (below) has been covered with a Gobelins-type fabric in saffron and black. Rich dark fabrics with elaborate patterns seem to go hand in hand with Victorian furniture, as do black frames.

OVERLEAF LEFT *In a Dutch farmhouse drawing room the doors of a large cabinet have been opened to reveal a display of earthenware tureens, plates and eighteenth-century blue-and-white china. The household linen would originally have been stored in the drawers below. Sandwiched between the cupboard and a side table bearing Staffordshire dogs is a metal campaign bed that has been turned into a comfortable chaise longue by the addition of a deep-buttoned soft mattress and a cushion covered in antique fabric. These antique military beds are not rare (there were too many wars to fight!) and the fact that they can be folded makes them ideal for storage and moving.*

OVERLEAF RIGHT *Frédéric Méchiche loves the Directoire style, and in the drawing room of his guest house in the south of France he has successfully combined pale lavender walls with engravings, furniture, a mirror and a lamp from his favourite period. The traditional pure wool carpet from Cogolin is contemporary and so is the classic footstool, but the contemporary-looking sofa with a ticking mattress cover and a set of plump, cream-coloured cushions is an antique metal Directoire bed. Méchiche chose it not only because of its period, but also because its simple lines have a timeless appeal.*

LEFT *Clutter has been kept to a minimum in Andrea Trulio's Neoclassical drawing room in Rome. Behind a chaise longue, upholstered in pale grey and equipped with striped cushions, stands a copy of a Roman table made of bronze and marble. It supports a pair of Italian Neoclassical marble vases and the plaster copy of a bust of the goddess Juno, which was bought at the sale of the storerooms of Cinecittà, the Italian answer to Hollywood. Plaster busts of ancient gods and goddesses abound, but it is not always easy to find good contemporary casts of this quality.*

RIGHT *The upstairs drawing room in Dennis Severs' former Huguenot silk weaver's house in London is crammed with period furniture, lamps, china, paintings and engravings. The look is one of cluttered cosiness. Severs reinstalled a period fireplace and panelling, which he painted an appropriate colour that hovers somewhere between* Cuisse de Nymphe *(Nymph's Thigh) and* Salmon. *Several manufacturers and specialist suppliers offer an extensive range of historical colours.*

OPPOSITE *Against a backdrop of pale blue, an eighteenth-century portrait of an Austrian officer, a painted drop-leaf table, an ormolu Louis XVI candlestick and a flowering geranium in a cylindrical, wooden container form a charming still life in a Dutch drawing room. Geraniums were very popular in the eighteenth-century interiors of northern Europe.*

THIS PAGE *The arrangement of an early nineteenth-century Porcelaine de Paris coffee pot with matching cup and saucer and sugar bowl on a metal Directoire guéridon, transforms this unadorned corner of a French drawing room into the essence of period elegance.*

DINING
ROOMS

'CONVIER QUELQU'UN, *c'est se charger de son bonheur pendant tout le temps qu'il est sous votre toit ...*' (To invite a guest means taking care of his well-being for as long as he is under your roof), wrote the Prince of Gastronomes, Anthelme Brillat-Savarin (1755-1826) in his *Physiologie du goût ou meditations de gastronomie transcendante.* By 'taking care' he meant not only treating guests to such delicacies as savoury quails *à la Talleyrand*, but also entertaining in a dining room worthy of his gastronomic delights. Unfortunately, Monsieur Brillat-Savarin's manners did not always match his stylish table. Some critics lamented his ability to drink twenty-two cups of coffee and gobble down twenty-two slices of buttered bread followed by a juicy steak, and his habit of wiping his hands on the hair of scantily dressed maids.

Our eating habits and dining-room etiquette have not always been the epitome of sophistication – quite the contrary. Before François I of France introduced forks to the dinner table in the sixteenth century,

PREVIOUS PAGES LEFT The table is inevitably the star in the dining room's decorative performance. French designer Patrice Gruffaz has turned the tiny entrance hall of his Paris flat into an elegant dining room with Directoire overtones by introducing a table covered with a generously draped linen tablecloth, twenties Neoclassical chairs and a striking faux white coral chandelier by Argentinian designer Roberto Bergero. Apart from the dinner service, there are no 'real' antiques in this room.

PREVIOUS PAGES RIGHT In a grand New York apartment, John Saladino has transformed the dining room into a realm of timeless beauty. Delicate hues of fawn, pale cream and the greyish-beige tone of natural linen fit this Neoclassical ensemble like a glove, and emphasize the elegance of the Roman-inspired mural and marble plinths.

everyone would try to grab the roasted capon's slithery leg with their bare hands. And even in seventeenth-century Holland, at the height of the Golden Age, the thick stems of the sturdy glass goblets from which wealthy burghers drank their Rhine wine were decorated with knobbly glass 'warts' to prevent their greasy fingers from losing their grip.

Nowadays our dining rooms are no longer filled with the type of scenes Hogarth depicted: jabbering dead-drunk gentlemen overturning the chairs and china punch bowls, and relieving themselves in a chamber pot in the corner of the room. Gone too are the days of the Grand Couvert at Versailles, where hundreds of people would watch the King dining with his family, and observe his menu and his table manners. Our modern etiquette is modelled on the nineteenth-century *service à la Russe.* These 'Russian' rules stipulated that only flowers and dessert should be displayed on the table, main courses should be served separately and in the right order, and plates returned directly to the kitchen after every course.

Just as the style of dining has changed over the centuries, so has the style of the dining room. The French painter Chardin's moving scenes of domestic life in the eighteenth century show us a humble table with a bread basket, some fruit, a knife and a pewter goblet. At the other end of the spectrum is novelist Restif de la Bretonne's romantic sketch of an eighteenth-century supper scene at the end of *The Age of Enlightenment,* which describes a most elegant table furnished with innumerable comforts and a centrepiece representing the three Graces, everything breathing an air of the most exquisite sensual pleasure.

An interesting description of a nineteenth-century ideal Victorian dining room is given in J.C. Loudon's *Encyclopaedia of Cottage, Farm and Villa Architecture and Furniture* (1833). The book mentions large logs burning in the hearth, with armchairs upholstered with crimson leather on either side of the fireplace, and a closet containing the smoking equipment and chamber pot required by the gentleman after dinner. In his *Suburban Gardener and Villa Companion* published five years later, Loudon proposed the installation of a 'speaking pipe' connecting the dining room with the kitchen, to allow the servants to whisper their orders to the cook downstairs.

Making a romantic dining room today requires a lot more than just candles, a starched tablecloth, monogrammed napkins and a dinner service inherited from Great-Aunt Elizabeth. Much depends on a neat eye and a rare talent for creating the right ambience. As the *éminence grise* of American decorators, John Saladino, puts it: 'God is in the details.' Those who have tried – and succeeded – know that the proportions of the room, the type of window and the choice of floorboards, carpeting, *tomettes* (terracotta tiles), marble or an antique parquet floor, are of the greatest importance. That is, if one wants to 'build' a dining room from scratch. But many people use an existing room – an extra bedroom, a large entrance hall, a scullery, or even a shed or barn.

This type of transformation happened in a late eighteenth-century manor house in Sweden, where an elegant dining room was born when a Gustavian square dining table was introduced in one of the empty anterooms, and a delicate, spidery crystal chandelier was hung from one of the ceiling beams. In a modest house in Normandy, a beautiful country dining room was created from a scullery when the walls were covered with red-and-white gingham, and the whole was cleverly completed by a wrought-iron, rustic chandelier, a rounded corner cupboard and a few earthenware tureens.

A splendid dining room in a chateau in France, which nowadays boasts wall panels decorated with Louis XVI garlands and an oversize table from the same period, was once an uninteresting entrance hall. A small dining room in a farm in the south of France, with its roughly plastered lavender-coloured walls, its powdery grey table and chairs and its pale pink *tomettes*, actually started its career as a pigsty. The entrance hall to a Parisian flat metamorphosed into a chic dining room complete with period chairs, period table and period chandeliers. Where once coats were hung and cabs were called, *boeuf bourguignon* is now eaten from delicate Empire plates and burgundy drunk from cut-crystal Directoire glasses. No one asks if the panelling is original, if there were always beams, or if the creaking parquet floor hides a platform of concrete. Who cares? The inhabitants just sit back and enjoy the ancestors' portraits, the set of engravings, the Georgian armchairs and the candlelight. After all, it's the magic that counts.

OVERLEAF LEFT In this vast dining room in a Beaux-Arts apartment building in New York, interior designer Anthony Lambert has drawn inspiration from the rather gloomy period details. Responding to the coffered ceiling, glazed doors and bow window, he enhanced the fin-de-siècle *atmosphere by introducing Liberty style wall coverings, an ormolu Art Nouveau chandelier and the dark dining-room furniture.*

OVERLEAF RIGHT It is almost impossible to tell that this positively Hogarthian dining room in Spitalfields, London, was decorated only a decade or so ago. The success of the venture is mainly due to the owner's exceptional knowledge of the Georgian style: Georgian armchairs, a period drop-leaf table, a crystal chandelier, an antique firegrate, and eighteenth-century silver and china stand out against glossy, dark-green panelling.

LEFT *Austerity reigns in this American dining room. A simple rush mat, a cabinet for storing and displaying silver and china, a large drop-leaf table, dining chairs and an austere Colonial armchair are the only items of furniture. The panelling is painted bronze and the painted plaster medallion represents George Washington.*

RIGHT ABOVE *In this elegant but spartan dining room created by Lars Sjöberg, the splendid floorboards were left uncovered, the walls whitewashed and a drop-leaf Swedish Rococo table and matching chair were given pride of place. The simple ladderback chairs are lined up against the walls when not in use, following eighteenth-century practice.*

RIGHT BELOW *Dutch interior designer Ischa van Delft and antiques dealer Jean-Jacques Massé drew inspiration from eighteenth-century American and Scandinavian interiors when they decorated the dining room of their nineteenth-century village house. The walls and ceiling were clad with tongue-and-groove panelling, which was then painted a pale blue-green.*

THIS PAGE *In Dutch designer Maroeska Metz's house in France, a former bedroom has become a dining room. The old-fashioned striped wallpaper is original, but the draped satin pelmets and matching curtains are new. The wrought-iron chandelier, table and chairs were designed by the owner (who also created her own china coffee and tea service). They may be modern additions, but they are perfectly in keeping with the period surroundings.*

OPPOSITE *In a house in Friesland in the northern Netherlands, a brand-new dining room has been created using period furnishings. The terracotta tiles on the newly laid floor are antique; so is the recently installed panelling. The eighteenth-century German cupboard was given new coats of red and blue paint, and the Empire-style dining chairs were upholstered in a typically nineteenth-century ticking stripe. The whole room looks as though it has existed for centuries.*

LEFT *The inside of a late eighteenth-century Basque cupboard has been painted Sèvres pink, and the plain shelves have been replaced by scalloped ones. Rare creil tureens, eighteenth- and nineteenth-century silver, miscellaneous crockery, candlesticks, Capodimonte figures and modern creamware form a surprisingly harmonious still life. Creamware in classical shapes is still produced today and is relatively inexpensive.*

RIGHT ABOVE *A recent re-edition of an eighteenth-century china dinner service graces the shelves of this built-in cupboard, which has been painted a warm red. Several manufacturers – Herend, Sèvres, K.P.M. Berlin and Limoges, for example – produce modern versions of their classic designs.*

RIGHT BELOW *An eighteenth-century Dutch cabinet has been crammed with the remaining pieces of a blue-and-white china tea service and with antique glasses. The long-stemmed 'genever' glasses would have been used on special occasions, such as wedding celebrations and funeral wakes.*

OVERLEAF LEFT *The dining room of a simple Dutch farmhouse has been decorated with suitable restraint, using only simple country furniture, such as an eighteenth-century Dutch painted cupboard, a round antique table and farmhouse chairs with rush seating. The crockery on the table is nineteenth-century, as are the glasses, cutlery, wicker bread-basket and winebottle holder. The glass-fronted cupboard on the right is used for storing glassware, crockery and china.*

OVERLEAF RIGHT *A collection of nineteenth-century white china tureens, fruit bowls, sauceboats and liqueur glasses of the same period and an original sugar cone are exhibited in the top of this cabinet. The subtle colour scheme of the display – pale Gustavian grey, white and black – is a successful exercise in monochromatic composition.*

KITCHENS

THE SEVENTEENTH-CENTURY DUTCH painters Pieter de Hooch, Johannes Vermeer, Gerard ter Borch and Jan Steen have left us some wonderfully detailed and inspiring kitchen scenes. Their dimly lit and moody interiors with shining marble floors, filled with highly polished brass kettles hanging from roasting jacks and earthenware jugs overflowing with rich, creamy milk transport us to the realm of the senses. We can almost smell the sweet aroma of golden-brown pancakes, hear the noise of the wings of struggling partridges brought back from the market in a wicker basket by a merciless maidservant, and taste the chilled white wine that a hostess pours from a silver-lidded Delft pitcher for a visiting officer.

Our eyes are constantly distracted by the interior details in genre scenes. When we look at Jean-Baptiste Oudry's illustration for La Fontaine's fable *The Swan and the Cook* – the tale of the drunken cook who is prevented from killing and roasting a swan by its beautiful 'swan song' – our attention is held not so much by the action as by the kitchen setting: the squared stone floor, solid wooden working table, cast-iron rack for hanging venison, shelves laden with sieves, skimmers, earthenware pots or a lonely brioche.

Historical houses and stately homes are also an endless source of inspiration. Sometimes they reveal fantasy on a huge scale: when Friedrich Wilhelm II of Prussia, nephew of Frederick the Great and successor to the throne, was planning the kitchen in his Marble Palace in Potsdam in 1787, he asked his architects Von Gontard and Langhans to give it the appearance of a ruined Greek temple. George IV's Regency kitchen at Brighton Pavilion is an astonishing cathedral-like space complete with palm-tree columns. Rows of pots and pans line the

PREVIOUS PAGES LEFT Antique objects arranged on kitchen shelves look most appealing when they are linked together by theme, style, period or colour. In this display inside a painted eighteenth-century cupboard, it is colour that acts as the unifying factor. A typically Dutch still life has been assembled using nineteenth-century crockery from the factory of Petrus Regoùt in Maastricht, antique tea towels, a paisley shawl, old fabrics and a few antique boxes. The whole composition is anchored by a nineteenth-century wicker linen basket filled with apples, and the blue of the cupboard forms a striking contrast to the dominant red of the objects inside.

PREVIOUS PAGES RIGHT In this kitchen, a tall cupboard dating from the nineteenth century has retained its original faux-bois *exterior finish and black interior. It forms an ideal background for a display of nineteenth-century Dutch earthenware and china. The inspiration for this arrangement clearly comes from the seventeenth-century Old Masters; even the way the table has been laden with crockery, food and cutlery is reminiscent of Dutch still lifes. Perhaps in homage to painterly* chiaroscuro, *a great deal of effort has gone into creating a subtle colour scheme consisting of dark brown, black, off-whites, cream and the natural tones of wood.*

walls, and there are an astonishing number of mechanical devices that once allowed the cook and his assistants to concoct gargantuan meals for hundreds of guests.

All over the world, curators of houses open to the public understand the popularity of kitchens. Visitors adore strolling through them, and they are equally curious about the larder, the butler's pantry and the housekeeper's sitting room. These quarters do not necessarily have to be grand: indeed there seems to be a greater appeal in the modest rooms below stairs than in the elegant morning room upstairs.

Many claim that they get the most accurate picture of everyday life in the old days while visiting the rooms in the basement with such time- and labour-consuming horrors as wringers, mincers, chopping-blocks, flour-sieves and coal-bunkers. Hearts start beating faster and plans are made to exchange unsightly lino for solid oak floorboards, to wash sterile white walls with a mixture of natural pigment and buttermilk, and to haunt country auctions and flea markets in search of that rare seventeenth-century colander, the earliest possible Regency jelly-mould or the remains of the genuine cottage stool with the rush seat.

We seem to be growing tired of the sterile laboratory-kitchen filled with the latest electronic equipment that is the height of fashion today, but will be discarded tomorrow. For many years now one of the most successful antiques shops in the Parisian Marché aux Puces has been a lofty space that resembles a romantic French country kitchen, where one can browse at leisure among stacks of bread-planks, rows of Provençal earthenware jugs and bowls, piles of old table linen, tea towels and aprons, copper *batteries de cuisine*, wicker baskets, antique wooden spoons, ladles, and knives and cast-iron cookers.

Ironically, what we admire in a romantic kitchen today is the result of our ancestors' craving for the latest development in kitchen equipment. If a Georgian housewife had been given the choice between a mechanical roasting rack from the 1780s or the latest hot-air oven, she would have chosen the latter without hesitation. And although our fascination with ancient kitchens is inevitably linked with our nostalgia for the unique ambience of a bygone era, there is a limit to our quest for authenticity. We realize that it is an ordeal to light the hearth, the stove and the furnace, and we absolutely refuse to scour copper pots and pans in the old-fashioned way or to cruelly fatten the chicken confined in a tiny basket with oatmeal balls and aniseed. Having turned our high-technology kitchens into realms of sheer beauty, we will probably stop short of sprinkling the floors of our cooking temples with saffron to prevent the cook from getting drunk, as the Romans did, or painting the walls that special shade of blue that was thought to repel flies in the eighteenth century.

What we really want is the atmosphere conjured up by the smoke-coloured walls, the uneven terracotta tiles and the glazed tureen that echoes the shape of a hare and seems to add extra flavour to our culinary efforts.

RIGHT ABOVE *In the kitchen of a late eighteenth-century house, a large pine cupboard has been crammed with earthenware crockery. Together with the plain pine table and chairs it evokes the simple pleasures of country life.*

RIGHT CENTRE *In this eighteenth-century American country house, the kitchen has miraculously remained untouched and the owner has accentuated the spareness of the room, with its whitewashed chimney breast and original floorboards, by introducing rustic country furniture and a pair of high-back Colonial chairs. The metal lantern is a Shaker design; lanterns of this type are still being produced.*

RIGHT BELOW *The Dutch obsession with cleanliness is legendary. In the kitchen of this typical Dutch Biedermeier town house, modern white marble floor tiles coexist with the original pristine white Delft ones on the walls. The fitted cupboards, also original to the kitchen, were painted blue by the owner because blue was a traditional colour for kitchens. It was also a standard colour for nineteenth-century enamelled metal kitchenware such as kettles, buckets and breadbins.*

OPPOSITE *The kitchen in Dutch antiques dealers Karel and Will Leenaer's shop is only a few years old, but the installation of antique flooring, fitted cupboards and shelves based on traditional kitchen furniture, and white Delft tiles on the walls has resulted in a room that looks deceptively authentic.*

OVERLEAF LEFT *It is perfectly possible to create new storage with a period look. In a French chateau, the owner has built fitted cupboards that resemble old larders with slatted doors, to house his crockery and linen. A large scrubbed pine table, nineteenth-century country chairs, an impressive set of copper pots and pans, a copper lantern, wicker baskets and glass storage jars all contribute to the illusion of authenticity. Modern versions of* batteries de cuisine, *traditional wicker baskets and old-fashioned glass storage jars are all widely available.*

OVERLEAF RIGHT *In a modest seventeenth-century town house in the Netherlands, part of a large room on the first floor has been turned into a kitchen. The space is partitioned off by a nineteenth-century painted screen decorated with hunting scenes. Hooks have been attached to the ancient beams so that baskets and jugs can be stored out of the way. Although many of the elements in this kitchen cannot strictly be called 'antiques', this room has an undeniably period ambience.*

LEFT *When Ute Middelhoek bought her early nineteenth-century village house – originally a church – there was only a primitive kitchen. She created a new one virtually from scratch, but gave it a period look by installing pine floorboards, panelling made from traditional tongue-in-groove planks, fitted cupboards for her antique crockery and glass, a nineteenth-century earthenware sink and an* oeil-de-boeuf *window to let in more light. A pine table, French country chairs and a nineteenth-century French lamp with a milk-glass shade and a porcelain pulley (copies of which are still being made today) are a perfect choice of furnishing. Nineteenth-century mercury glass sits on top of the oak sideboard.*

RIGHT ABOVE *A nineteenth-century cupboard has been painted ox-blood red – a traditional paint (still available today) that uses the natural oxidation of iron and is reputed to curb woodworm. A charming and painterly still life has been made inside by filling the shelves with piles of antique tea towels, and an antique wicker basket overflowing with canvas and ribbons. The beauty of this trompe-l'oeil arrangement owes a great deal to the subtle colour scheme of cream and rusty red, and to the deceptively casual way in which the items are stored.*

RIGHT BELOW *On the shelves of an eighteenth-century Dutch kitchen cupboard is a display of rare Dutch travelling cases made of* Bois de Spa *(eighteenth-century plywood), decorated with pastoral scenes and arabesques.*

LEFT *The colours in Jean and Dorothée d'Orgeval's kitchen in Roussillon, in the south of France, echo the warm glow of the red ochre hills surrounding their house. Dorothée mixed local red earth with beeswax to create the soft sheen on the walls. The room was then furnished with nineteenth-century farmhouse furniture made locally. Provençal earthenware plates, trays, pots and other kitchen utensils line the walls or are placed in niches.*

OVERLEAF LEFT *The kitchen in the house that once belonged to Dutch writer Betje Wolff (1738-1804) has been reconstructed with meticulous care so that it looks as it might have done in her day. The white Delft tiles and impressive hearth are authentic, but since none of the original furnishings or kitchen utensils remained, the room was completed with a table, chairs, china, period brass and an antique high chair supplied by admirers of her work. The valance below the mantelpiece is made from the striped fabric still used for traditional Dutch costumes, which is sold in a few specialist shops in the Netherlands.*

OVERLEAF RIGHT *A colourful valance and a symmetrical composition of nineteenth-century china, candelabra and a richly embroidered antique tea cosy, have turned the hood of this fireplace into the equivalent of a Victorian display cabinet. The Victorian cast-iron cooker is original to the flat, which stands in the shadow of Edinburgh Castle.*

LIBRARIES
AND
STUDIES

IN HIS *Suburban Gardener and Villa Companion* of 1838, J.C. Loudon – who was never short of good advice – wrote that the decoration of a library should form a strong contrast with the more light-hearted elegance of the drawing room. The colour of the walls should be dark, and there should be two or three armchairs equipped with pivoting reading stands. In Loudon's time, the library was generally used as the gentleman's morning room and ladies – although mildly tolerated – were not encouraged to install themselves in this temple of masculine superiority. More than a quarter of a century later, Robert Kerr in *The Gentleman's House* advised the cultivated man to isolate himself from the household behind double doors, making sure that the library became his private retreat. A nineteenth-century library was a man's world, and it was not done for a woman to disturb her male companion's peace of mind by bursting into the inner sanctum uninvited. Fortunately, this is no longer the case.

Surrounding ourselves with favourite books, collecting rare specimens, first editions, manuscripts, the odd Egyptian papyrus roll or an autographed letter by Nelson or Mata Hari can be an irresistible urge. One does not have to be a bookworm to be seduced by the dry, dusty, leathery smell of books. Rows of books, shelves that almost collapse under the weight of knowledge and impressive bookcases crammed with the printed word have our unconditional devotion.

We collect books avidly, we raid brand-new and second-hand bookshops, we run to auctions and steal feverishly along the banks of the River Seine in the hope of discovering new treasures. Or – worse – we search the dustbins and the skips at night for that eighteenth-century binding embossed with gold or that unique manuscript that has been discarded furiously by a disenchanted and desperate poet.

Sometimes a shock lies in store. The French writer Colette stopped collecting old books when she came home from the *bouquiniste's* one day with an extremely rare Balzac volume and found a revoltingly filthy comb between its pages, probably left there by some absent-minded collector who had used it as a bookmark. The poet Goethe, on the other hand, could not survive without his favourite books within reach, and because he was an inveterate collector, he even moved a modest part of his library to his garden house, where he would retire for long periods to write, seated on the strangely shaped high stool he called his *sitz-bock* (goat-seat).

Those who wish to recreate period libraries have plenty of images to choose from. There is the medieval chamber, with its bearded hermit bending over a pile of manuscripts; or the Rembrandtesque room, filled with a large oak table, bulky scientific reference works, a yellowing human skull, an incidental stuffed owl and a terrestrial globe. Our imaginations may be fired by the image of an eighteenth-century bookcase, proudly displaying ox-blood 'maroquin' binding with embossed gold coats of arms and refined *objets-de-vertu*, or the idea of a sophisticated Regency study featuring a dandy reading a novel with one arm resting against the marble mantelpiece. Or we might be tempted to make a cosy Victorian library, which seems to embody our ancestors' (and our own) craving for knowledge, with its fitted shelves and bookcases filled from floor to ceiling with old volumes, a tartan Axminster carpet, deep-buttoned armchairs covered in dried-out, cracked leather and a few softly glowing oil lamps.

Nowadays there is nothing to stop us from fulfilling our period fantasies. Everything is within reach: the antique hour glass, the old map, the faded engravings and the masses of books are only waiting to be assembled and turned into an image of haunting beauty.

PREVIOUS PAGES LEFT *In one of the rooms of Hörle Herrgård, a manor house in the south of Sweden, Lars Sjöberg has put together the perfect eighteenth-century study.*
PREVIOUS PAGES RIGHT *The study at Schiller's Weimar residence has been carefully reconstructed, and features a still life consisting of old books, a period clock and candlestick, a reproduction of the poet's glass ink-well and a terrestrial globe.*

LEFT *A room in an eighteenth-century French manor house has been turned into a library by its owner, who installed old bookcases and shelving that exactly fitted the spaces either side of the fireplace, and placed a robust, nineteenth-century writing desk in the middle of the room. The antique volumes are part of his extensive collection of books and manuscripts, and the wallpaper is a modern reprint of a period document (many wallpaper manufacturers produce reprinted historical papers). The lamps are also modern, and the bust on the mantel is a copy of a nineteenth-century original.*

RIGHT *Paris antiques dealer Serge Hubert has turned his tiny sitting room into a library by incorporating fitted bookcases and shelves into the period panelling. The shelves are artistically overstuffed with books and objets d'art. Everything, including the furniture, dates from the nineteenth century.*

LEFT *In a French chateau, one of the rooms on the first floor has been turned into a library by the installation of a large bookcase, a table covered with an antique kilim and a set of Louis XV armchairs covered in ancient embossed velvet. Masses of precious and leather-bound books, a marble bust, a sturdy library ladder and a colour scheme of warm, earthy tones create a welcoming atmosphere.*

RIGHT *Carefully arranged still lifes of classical statues, prints and drawings can add a sense of drama to a study or library. They do not have to be originals: plaster casts of classical statuary can be obtained from museum shops and good reproductions of architectural drawings are available from contemporary print dealers. In his study (top), a French antiques dealer has grouped an eighteenth-century architectural drawing, nineteenth-century oil lamps and antique plaster casts of Greek and Roman statuary on top of a nineteenth-century commode.*

Another study (centre) has been given a distinctive, intellectual air by a well-displayed collection of nineteenth-century and Neoclassical bronzes, a row of books and a table with a top of inlaid marble.

French interior designer Guy Thorodoff's nineteenth-century ballroom (below) has been successfully converted into a fin-de-siècle *study which incorporates some of the decorative elements popular at that time: a terracotta portrait bust, a lamp crowned by a shade made from shirred fabric, old leather-bound books and a neo-Renaissance table clock.*

OVERLEAF LEFT *Bookcases and library shelves are given added interest when the books are artfully arranged and interspersed with prints and all sorts of precious (and less precious) decorative objects. The addition of the silver scale-model of a boat and a pair of beautifully framed, hand-painted miniature portraits (top left) is perfectly in keeping with the luxurious, Napoleon III-style library in this Paris apartment.*

Framed, antique prints, paintings and watercolours, an antique candlestick, a precious vase and an etched portrait of an eighteenth-century gentleman in an oval frame (top right and bottom left) can turn a few shelves or the top of a bookcase into an intriguing collector's cabinet.

Frédéric Méchiche has adorned his library (bottom right) with a Ptolemaic mask and an eighteenth-century Italian giltwood mirror, adding cultural diversity to the rows of books.

OVERLEAF RIGHT *The seventeenth-century Dutch and Flemish masters provided inspiration for this trompe l'oeil still life. A nineteenth-century copy of a seventeenth-century Dutch ebonized frame was placed in front of a few bookshelves containing precious, inlaid boxes, a mounted ostrich egg, a string of pearls, books and documents, and the 'lemon with corkscrew peel' – a traditional element in paintings of the Golden Age.*

BEDROOMS

DECORATING A BEDROOM is not always an easy task – too many bedrooms display an astonishing lack of imagination. The frightening drabness of so many hotel rooms is a perfect example: a naked lightbulb, a washbasin, a plain bed hidden under a worn bedspread and the horror is complete. Put a corpse on the bed, let in the famous Inspector Maigret and you have a fine start for a *film noir*.

Anyone with a spark of romance would prefer to sleep in a refined giltwood Louis XVI bed in the purest Marie-Antoinette style, in a panelled room painted Trianon grey, where the drapes, eiderdown, pillows and bolsters are made of celadon damask silk. The idea of a heavy Victorian four-poster made of solid oak, with twisted columns and a feather-light quilted duvet is equally seductive. As is the notion

PREVIOUS PAGES LEFT *One can safely indulge a love of fabric and pattern in bedroom decoration. The off-white walls in this house in the south of France provide an ideal neutral background for the strawberry-coloured toile de Jouy used for the bedhangings and the chair. Swathes of this imposing fabric have transformed a modest bedroom into an apparently genuine eighteenth-century bedchamber.*

PREVIOUS PAGES RIGHT *In the bedroom of a nineteenth-century house in Paris, the owners have created a sophisticated mood using subtle variations of the same tone. Cream-coloured walls and mouldings set off a Louis XV-style nineteenth-century fireplace made of cream marble and a faux Louis XV caned bed. The bed and chair are both painted* caca d'oie *(goosedropping), a favourite colour for furniture around 1900 as a result of the Louis XVI revival.*

of spending the night in the guest room of a house overlooking the Mediterranean, under a billowing mosquito net made of the finest muslin, with a gentle breeze flowing through the open French windows.

We have come a long way since our Cro-Magnon ancestors huddled together in caves under layers of fur, seeking shelter against the ever-threatening night and the elements. Since then, beds and bedrooms have undergone many transformations. The Egyptians were the first to introduce sophistication to sleeping arrangements, employing their talented carpenters and goldsmiths to create sumptuous reclining beds for their divine pharaohs. The Romans tried to do better. As they could never really make up their minds where to sleep in their luxurious Pompeian villas, they had beds in every room.

In medieval times, beds became splendid affairs, often draped in rich velvets and brocades. They can be seen in some Flemish 'primitive' paintings showing 'bath-house' or brothel scenes, where a happy company of naked gentlemen as white as the sheets and their equally pale ladies recline on the bed under a canopy of crimson cloth. Later came the tester beds with fringed curtains that we observe in the darkest corners of the Dutch interiors painted by Vermeer or Pieter de Hooch, and the Baroque constructions with coronets of feathers on each of the four corners, built during the reigns of William and Mary and the Sun King. Beds with canopies have long been popular. Perhaps this is because we are suffering from nostalgia for the maternal womb and have an irresistible urge to adorn our 'nests' with a hood, or at least overhead protection.

Montaigne once declared, 'I prefer a beautiful bed to a comfortable bed.' His words help explain the appeal of the *lit d'apparat*, the ostentatious bed designed purely for show, and draped with rich velvets and silks, which seems to be making a comeback. But sensational effects can also be achieved with less opulent fabrics – for example, the toile de Jouy invented by Monsieur d'Oberkampf, who charmed his eighteenth-century contemporaries with a printed cotton that showed raspberry-coloured pastoral scenes by Jean-Baptiste Huet on an off-white background. Or the bed can be draped with flimsy muslin to bring freshness in the sweltering heat of a tropical climate. Or it can be shrouded in gingham – preferably blue-and-white – which seems to be the trademark of Scandinavian homes, where the winters are long and cold, and no bedroom is complete without an earthenware stove.

The people who have created the bedrooms in this chapter are – without exception – romantic souls. They have whitewashed their walls or painted them with layers of transparent wash made of natural pigments. They have covered them with fabric (old or seemingly old) or with old-fashioned wallpaper and they have stippled, rag-rolled, marbled, frescoed, trompe l'oeiled, stencilled or panelled them to create the illusion of a period room.

Some have simple tastes. In a quiet and rural setting, in an old farmhouse with sash windows, wooden floorboards and inside shutters, the bedroom will harbour a simple wooden bed or one made of brass and wrought-iron. It will be covered with a checked plaid or a striped coverlet and the sheets – starched and crisp – will be the purest linen. There might be a washstand with an earthenware pitcher and bowl, a vase that holds an unpretentious bunch of dried flowers and an armchair hiding under a floppy slipcover with a floral print and a cushion embroidered with a personal memento.

On the other hand, bedrooms inspired by the past can be an expression of extravagant fantasy, devised to mislead the beholder. The grandest of bedchambers that looks as though it belongs in a centuries-old manor might be found in a modest city dwelling. A tiny apartment might boast the most frivolous marquis's retreat full of bows and frills. Pastel-coloured Biedermeier sleeping quarters could be found in a one-bedroom flat in a high-rise block, behind lace curtains that hide a skyscraper landscape. The only limits are those of the imagination.

OVERLEAF LEFT Bed hangings provide further opportunities for using pattern, whether it be in extravagantly gathered curtains or restricted to panels and borders. In this splendid Normandy bedroom – which was literally conjured out of nothing, using salvaged architectural elements – the same fabric has been used for the bed and wall coverings, following eighteenth-century taste. It is Papillons, Philippe La Querrière's modern edition of an old pattern.

OVERLEAF RIGHT A period four-poster dominates this bedroom in an American country house. The interior designer, James Joseph, has followed another eighteenth-century custom in using simple bed hangings to provide a neutral background for a more elaborate and colourful bedspread and pillows.

LEFT *Some rustic settings call for simple bed treatments. Antiques dealers Arno Verhoeven and Jaap Eckhardt ransacked the Dutch countryside to get hold of their favourite Friesian Biedermeier ticking stripe for one of the guest rooms of their farmhouse. Ticking was originally used to cover old mattresses and duvet covers, and is still made by many modern manufacturers. The bed has been stencilled with a garland pattern, and the Laura Ashley Réveillon wallpaper has been given a delicate blue wash. Arno decorated the medallion of the Louis XVI-style fire-screen with a romantic bouquet and painted the floorboards and the door in traditional Dutch colours.*

RIGHT *Stylist Hugo Curletto found this nineteenth-century Spanish bed with a carved headboard in the barn of his house in northern Spain. He gave the bedroom's whitewashed walls a blue wash (using natural indigo pigment mixed with buttermilk and water) and drew the trompe l'oeil cornice. He also had the clever idea of fastening the top of a flimsy mosquito net to the antique chandelier above the bed.*

RIGHT AND FAR RIGHT BELOW
Using the skills he developed when teaching painting techniques, Arno Verhoeven painstakingly decorated the walls of this bedroom with an astonishing trompe l'oeil copy of a Biedermeier wallpaper from Schloss Corvey in Germany. The wallpaper represented swags of elaborately draped, striped fabric (so typical of the reigning taste in early nineteenth-century Germany) and was manufactured using a block-print technique, so Arno imitated exactly the several stages of printing by hand. This decorative drudgery took him almost two years to finish. Subsequently the bed was crowned with a canopy of draped fabric and covered with a checked, blue-and-white Indian bedspread. All the furniture and the objects in this room are Biedermeier pieces, from Holland and Germany.

FAR RIGHT ABOVE *Frédéric Méchiche often makes use of antique fabrics when he decorates a house, and for the bedroom in this modestly proportioned guest house in the south of France he chose to dress up the modern bed with an antique Provençal quilted coverlet, antique linen sheets (which he used for the bed hangings and curtains) and a few yards of eighteenth-century, striped, blue-and-white fabric.*

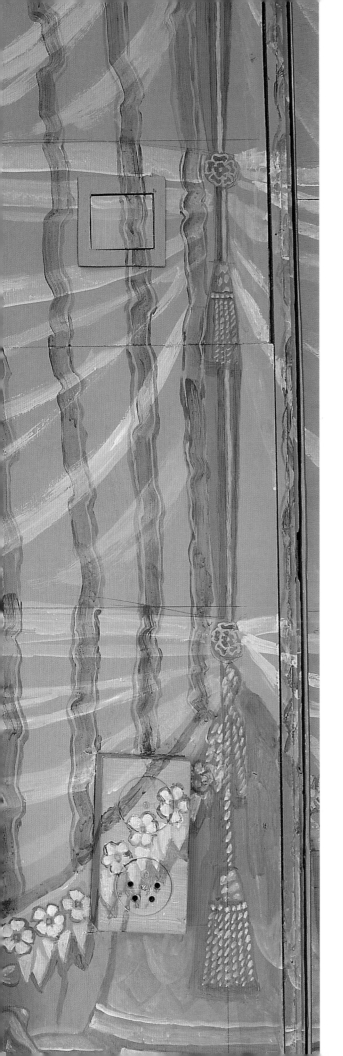

LEFT *A sturdy nineteenth-century bed dominates the bedroom of an American country house. The antique bedspread and coverlet are in keeping with the room's rustic feel, while the original finish of the whitewashed walls, the unadorned beams and peeling paintwork has been left undisturbed.*

RIGHT *Belgian interior designer Benoît Vliegen designed this robust, traditional Swiss pine bed following an eighteenth-century pattern, striving to create perfect harmony between the bed and the antique pitch-pine panelling that he installed in the bedroom of this modern Swiss chalet apartment. The bed linen was chosen for its unsophisticated, rustic qualities and so were the rest of the furnishings: a wall-light with a* rocaille *ornament, an antique wall sconce and an old painted Swiss armoire.*

RIGHT *The* lit d'apparat – *or show bed – seems to be making a comeback. Jean and Dorothée d'Orgeval have installed one – a seventeenth-century four-poster bed – at the far end of their barn in the south of France. The antique bed hangings, the period plumes on the four corners of the bed and the eighteenth-century Provençal quilted coverlet all complement the grandeur of this genuine 'state bed', the faded yellow of the fabrics forming a striking contrast with the dark oak of the headboard and the pale terracotta of the tiled floor. An eighteenth-century Provençal* duchesse brisée *(literally 'a broken duchess', meaning an armchair with a matching footstool) is covered with a kilim plaid. Kilims are inexpensive, and their wonderful colours and patterns can form a strong focal point in an uncluttered interior with a serene colour scheme.*

FAR RIGHT ABOVE *A spectacular eighteenth-century Indian silver four-poster from the palace of a Maharaja now graces a Paris bedroom. A sumptuous bedspread embroidered with gold and silver thread, antique bed hangings, a portrait of a bejewelled Indian sovereign and a matching silver footstool turn this bedroom into a vision from Sheherazade's* Thousand and One Nights.

FAR RIGHT BELOW *Jacques Garcia has assembled a modern version of a perfect period bedroom by introducing an antique carpet and Louis XV armchair and by draping the original alcove and modern bed with luxurious old fabrics.*

BEDROOMS

THIS PAGE AND OPPOSITE *Period bed linen and antique textiles naturally lend themselves to decorative display. On the shelves of an old armoire (right) piles of quilted coverlets, embroidered fabrics, lace, toile de Jouy and chintz create a riot of contrasting textures and colours. Tassels and ribbons can also provide ornamental touches with a period feel. A scarlet satin pin cushion has been hung with deliberate nonchalance on the handle of an eighteenth-century door (below), while the key in an old Dutch cupboard has been embellished with a tassel (right above), and the lock of a Directoire door is secured with an antique tie-back made from a rope and tassels (right below).*

OVERLEAF LEFT *Ute Middelhoek has created a cosy attic bedroom by filling it with nineteenth-century furniture – a French metal bed and a Dutch faux-bois chest of drawers – and an attractive selection of china, quilts and bed linen.*

OVERLEAF RIGHT *The exposed beams in Patricia Padberg's Dutch town house reminded her of an ancient farm building, so she furnished the attic bedroom in the rustic style, equipping it with an iron and brass bed, and antique and modern bed linen.*

BATHROOMS

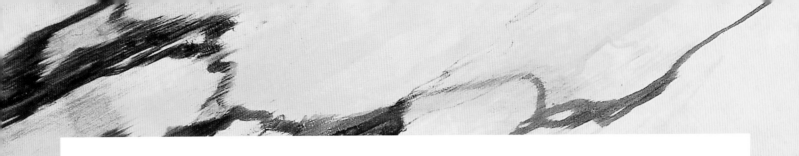

O F ALL THE ROOMS IN THE HOUSE, bathrooms are the greatest fun to decorate. A bathroom presents endless opportunities to indulge the imagination, and there are so many possibilities and styles, so many shapes of bath and such a mass of accessories, tiles and furniture available that it is often hard to make a choice. We might want to echo the style of our ancestors' elaborate canopied bathtubs, the walls stencilled with swags and garlands, or the marble slabs, soft carpets or smooth parquet floors that once represented the height of fashion. Taking inspiration from the past, we can let our minds wander freely from the oriental look to a

PREVIOUS PAGES In his Paris apartment, Frédéric Méchiche has conjured up the illusion of a perfect Directoire-style bathroom using a mixture of fakery and original pieces. In one corner he has turned a period console table into a washstand by setting a bowl into a marble top and adding period sanitary fittings. Early tôle oil lamps have been electrified, and the walls given a sepia-grey wash to make them resemble the colour of ancient stucco. Standing on a plinth is a nineteenth-century terracotta bust, based on Houdon's well-known masterpiece La Frileuse. *Modern comforts have not been neglected: the period doors hide a well-equipped modern shower. A Directoire copper bath on a raised stone plinth is complemented by the lead cistern in a shallow niche above it. Swags of white muslin pick up the pale colours in the stone floor inlaid with black cabochons. The room's rounded corners have been adorned with panels of nineteenth-century grisaille wallpaper, printed by Dufour and still available today. The Neo-classical columns are topped with capitals that Méchiche had specially cast in resin.*

pinkish boudoir, or from a Neoclassical scheme with busts of emperors and a sunken bath fit for a *femme fatale* to an intimate Victorian affair with palms and heavily fringed curtains.

Attitudes to bathrooms have varied enormously over the centuries, just as bathing has gone in and out of fashion. We know that Henri IV of France was nicknamed 'The Goat', on account of his poor hygiene. And according to legend, the only woman at Louis XV's court who bathed regularly was Madame du Barry, who immersed herself in icy cold water twice a day. Daily ablutions were certainly not always appreciated by Napoleon, whose tiny handwritten note to his beloved wife Josephine – '*Je viens, ne te lave pas*' (I am coming . . . do not bathe) – is jealously guarded in a display cabinet in a French museum. Yet bathing has also been the subject of erotic tantalization: seventeenth-century engravings depict beautifully dressed 'ladies of quality' at their *levée* receiving their admirers while their maid indulges in the ceremony of washing their feet.

The Classical world had highly developed hygienic rituals. The ancient Greeks had a unique way of ridding themselves of the dust and sand from the streets of Athens by rubbing their bodies with oil and then scraping off the dirt with a special knife, or 'strigil'. But the Romans, who probably thought such a practice barbaric, adored contact with water. It was their belief in *Mens sana in corpore sano* (a healthy spirit in a clean body) that led to the invention of the bathroom and sophisticated plumbing to provide hot and cold water for bathing. In Emperor Caracalla's *thermae* thousands of people bathed together at the same time. It is an amusing coincidence that a pair of granite, oversized bathtubs from his 'bath-o-drome' have been turned into fountains and stand on the Piazza Farnese in Rome, opposite the convent of the Brigittines. If the sweet nuns knew where 'their' fountains came from, they would blush in modesty.

Perhaps it is not surprising that the Roman theme is a perennial favourite for bathroom decoration. We seem to see ourselves as Neros and Poppaeas, and fantasize about bathing in ass's milk. One of the most famous examples of this type of bathroom was designed in Paris in the late eighteenth century, when the famous architect François-Joseph Belanger built a splendid Neoclassical house for the scandalous dancer and *grande horizontale* Mademoiselle Dervieux. Belanger decorated the bathroom with exquisite Pompeiian motifs and cartouches reminiscent of the Greek Attic vases, whose terracotta figures on a black background were considered the epitome of good taste. Mademoiselle Dervieux was so pleased with the work of her architect that she subsequently married him. This is only a conclusion, not a hint.

We might have a liking for Palladian splendour, feel lured by Antiquity with its profusion of columns and statuary, or have a certain affinity with the elegant shapes that were born during the reign of Louis XV. Or a taste for all things simple and rural might lead us to make a modest bathroom with scrubbed floor-boards, a zinc hip-bath and a wooden towel rack. Anything goes – there are really no rules and no limits. The creative among us will not shy away from decorating the walls of our bathrooms with frescoes, from distressing layers of paint and stucco to get that mellowed Florentine look or from running beeswax on a coat of matt emulsion to turn it into a simplified version of *stucco antico*.

We hide ugly tiles behind panelling and early nineteenth-century wallpaper by Dufour. We scour the flea markets in search of a copper Directoire bath (and the matching 'swans' necks' taps), a copy of a Roman tripod and a Neoclassical X-shaped stool. We go in search of that peeling, rickety 'Swedish' table covered with the remains of smoky grey paint and the indispensible peeling, rickety washstand that make the bathroom with the muslin-draped window and the red geranium on the windowsill look so Gustavian.

We go to these extraordinary lengths because our bathrooms are the sanctuaries to which we retire after a busy day in the cruel world outside. Nancy Lancaster captured this sense of solace and retreat in her description of her bathroom in the coach house at Haseley Court, a lovely Queen Anne House in Oxfordshire: 'My favourite room in the Coach House is my bathroom . . . I use a chest of drawers as my dressing-table; its drawers are all painted Cambridge blue. All over the walls are huge white frames with blue paper on which I have made collages of photographs from my Kodak books. I lie in my bath and look at all the favourite people and places in my life spread out before me . . . '

We can only dream while reading these lines and try to borrow inspiration for our own bathrooms from their evocation of timeless elegance.

PAGE 140 *There are so many possibilities when it comes to wall decoration in the bathroom. An old-fashioned toile de Jouy wallpaper has been left on the walls of the bathroom next to the master bedroom in Maroeska Metz's French country retreat. Antique furniture, found in the attic, was painted blue to match the wallpaper and to complement Maroeska's own designs – the candlestick, mirror, chandelier and towel-rack. A late nineteenth-century zinc bath has been embellished with curly legs to match.*

PAGE 141

TOP LEFT *Italian interior designer Stefano Mantovani has covered his bathroom walls with white, octagonal tiles to provide a neutral foil for a daring mix of Neoclassical objects,* fin-de-siècle *furniture and Romantic paintings.*

TOP RIGHT *Jacques Garcia has created a late nineteenth-century ambience by painting his walls in two tones to suggest dado and panelling, and decorating them with an array of Victorian knick-knacks.*

BOTTOM LEFT *An extensive collection of framed drawings and engravings looks most effective against the plain walls of this French bathroom. The reproduction bathtub, resting on traditional claw-and-ball feet, has been painted the same colour as the walls.*

BOTTOM RIGHT *Inspired by the Classical world, Riccardo Cinalli has used his skills as a trompe l'oeil artist in his London bathroom to suggest fragments of antique fresco and an inlaid marble floor.*

OPPOSITE *In the bathroom of his Paris flat, Jean-Luc Gauzère has borrowed some elements from the traditional print room, covering the walls and doors with period engravings. It is easy to imagine one of Balzac's heroes performing his daily ablutions in this severe and masculine room, inspecting his image in the giltwood Empire mirror, surrounded by early nineteenth-century furniture and objects, and period linen.*

LEFT ABOVE *A bath has been cunningly fitted into an arched niche and clad with slabs of travertine marble (both real and faux) in this Parisian bathroom. Two mirrors on facing walls reflect endless images of carefully chosen accessories.*

LEFT CENTRE *A romantic bathroom has been created by generously draping a wall with pristine, white muslin. It provides a dramatic backdrop for the elaborately carved* fin-de-siècle *washstand – made of white marble and pale wood – and for the nineteenth-century 'Dagobert' chair, wooden towel-rack and period accessories.*

LEFT BELOW *An antique marble-topped washstand, still equipped with its original taps, gives this otherwise contemporary bathroom a charmingly retrospective feel. The modern tiles have been arranged in a pattern that reflects early twentieth-century taste.*

LEFT *Cupboards and panelling can create a variety of moods, from the luxurious to the functional. In a guest room in his Amsterdam apartment, American trompe l'oeil virtuoso Jay Henry Kester has created a washing area in a shallow built-in cupboard by installing an old-fashioned porcelain sink and taps, a salvaged slab of marble and a weathered mirror. The paint on the doors and panelling has been distressed to accentuate the 'authentic' look of the installation.*

RIGHT *Solid mahogany panelling lends an unmistakably masculine, Edwardian air to this London bathroom. The stone floor is a perfect complement to the severe decorative scheme. The obelisk – the only purely decorative element in the room – is a modern replica from the famous Manufacture de Sèvres.*

OVERLEAF *Architect James Joseph has equipped the bathroom in his American country house with a fitted closet that is in perfect harmony with the almost Shaker-like simplicity of the room. It serves as the ideal backdrop for an antique American chest and chair (left). The bath has been installed in a shallow alcove, and the back wall covered with a large panel of greyish marble (right). The theme of spartan simplicity is continued in the plain nineteenth-century table equipped with a porcelain washbasin, and the scrubbed wooden floorboards.*

GARDEN ROOMS

When Queen Christina of Sweden visited the late Cardinal Alessandro II Farnese's garden at Caprarola near Viterbo in the late seventeenth century, she was so impressed by the pagan beauty of Pietro Bernini's caryatids in the Casino Garden that she uttered the words: *Je n'ose prononcer ici le nom de Jésus, de crainte de rompre le charme'* ('I dare not pronounce the name of Jesus in this spot, for fear of breaking the enchantment'). And the Queen had a point, for despite the fact that Bernini's *canephorae* were placed there in 1620, the statues were part of a far more ancient heathen tradition of garden embellishment dating back to the Roman Empire. Today, visitors to the gardens of the Emperor Hadrian's villa at Tivoli can stare in disbelief at the ruins of a marble colonnade, at a handful of marble gods and at a singular and rather disturbing stone crocodile, whose presence in such august company strikes the same note as a modern garden gnome. The Romans clearly sometimes enjoyed flaunting their bad taste.

The Italian love of garden decoration illustrates the assertion made by the famous Dutch architect Sybold van Ravesteyn that we all have a natural longing for ornament. He believed that given the choice between a plain marble and one with a coloured twist we would invariably choose the latter. Louis XIV and his inspired garden architect André Le Nôtre would have agreed wholeheartedly with this theory. Versailles is, after all, the world's largest open-air sculpture museum, and there must be more petrified gods and goddesses in the gardens of the Sun King than there are in the Classical pantheon.

One of the great pleasures of the French monarch (apart from chasing young nymphs behind the bushes of his *domaine*) was organizing sumptuous garden fetes, mainly to draw his courtiers to Versailles and to keep them there. For these special events his servants would decorate the gardens with elaborate architectural constructions, building towering pyramids to support structures of marzipan, caramels and flowers and embellishing the grounds with statuary, giltwood *torchères*, chandeliers, columns, fountains and orange trees that bore preserved fruit. It may have been excessive, but it launched a fashion for garden decoration that had lain dormant since the Renaissance.

When the exiled French architect Daniel Marot was commissioned by William III to redecorate the castle and the gardens of Paleis Het Loo in the Netherlands, he shrewdly 'borrowed' designs for the garden urns from unknown sculptors and turned them into engravings, which he later published in a book which gained international fame and recognition. Dutch formal gardens owe a lot to the ornamental vocabulary of this clever Huguenot. And in the gardens of the rich merchants in the Hague and Amsterdam and the manicured grounds of the nobility throughout the perfectly flat countryside, Baroque vases, imposing arched pergolas, gazebos, tea pavilions, gilt sundials and marble busts on *rocaille* plinths representing the Four Seasons bloomed as never before. The rest of the world was soon slavishly following the trend.

PREVIOUS PAGES LEFT *In the garden room of a Dutch country house, a collection of old terracotta pots and wicker baskets arranged on the shelves of an antique cupboard create a pleasant, almost monochrome still life. Old terracotta pots often have interesting shapes since they have generally been thrown by hand and not cast in a mould. Nowadays, good reproductions, often imported from Italy, can be found at garden centres.*
PREVIOUS PAGES RIGHT *A romantic, intimate outdoor room has been created on a modest roof terrace in the heart of old Amsterdam. A table, a wicker armchair and masses of potted plants are set against trailing (and trained) ivy and whitewashed brick walls.*

From William Chambers' description in *The Garden and Buildings at Kew in Surry* (1763), it is clear that eighteenth-century gardens contained as many buildings, statues and monuments as trees and shrubs. The Georgians loved nature and the 'natural' landscape style made fashionable by Capability Brown, but they needed their strolls through gardens and parks to be interrupted at regular intervals by an inspiring vision of some Neoclassical temple or fake ruin. 'What was once a Desart is now an Eden', wrote Chambers, and of the twenty-odd constructions he described in Kew Gardens there were at least eight temples, a ruin, a mosque, a Gothic building, a Chinese Pavilion, a House of Confucius and 'a semi-octagon seat designed by Mr. Kent'.

On the other hand, Jean-Jacques Rousseau's back-to-nature philosophy was to inspire a taste for the simple and pastoral. Marie-Antoinette had a 'modest' cluster of cottages with thatched roofs erected in the shadow of her Trianon – Le Moulin Hameau – where she played at being a shepherdess in silk tending a flock of spotless sheep. And the illustrations in William Wright's *Grotesque Architecture and Rural Ornament* (1790) reflect perfectly the late eighteenth-century craze for bizarre grottoes and other Hansel-and-Gretel-like pavilions that would be the pride and joy of modern Disneylands. The taste for garden exotica ran riot: the eccentric Frederick the Great, King of Prussia and 'male muse' of Voltaire, insisted on installing a Chinese pagoda in his garden at Sanssouci and on adding several groups of heavily gilt statues of Chinamen to give his garden an extra oriental touch.

In the nineteenth century, the advent of industrialization and mass production meant that even the tiniest garden could boast a conservatory, a set of cast-iron benches that looked like an artistic jumble of branches, or a pair of oversized Medici vases holding spiky dracaenas. Gardens increasingly became fields for experiments and fantasy inspired by the great civilizations. The Victorians created Japanese gardens, Egyptian gardens and tropical gardens. They decorated them with orangeries, hothouses, aviaries, 'Roman' bathhouses and even the odd mausoleum. And several reckless garden-owners combined different styles without raising any eyebrows.

All these elements can provide excellent material for those who want to create a 'period' garden today. Indeed, one wonders what we would do without these fragments of history. Where would we be without the moss-covered obelisk or the ancient statue of Hebe that nowadays adorns the rose garden? Or how would the crumbling niche in the old brick wall near the kitchen garden look without the remains of an eighteenth-century urn? Today a rusty gate leading to the parterre with a clipped boxwood hedge is no longer replaced by a modern copy, and the gazebo that has seen better days will not be razed to the ground. We cherish the patina and the romance of the old shed with the gothic window that has long lost its coloured glass window panes. We are cautious about destruction now, for we have finally become the guardians of our past.

OVERLEAF Keith Skeel added a modern conservatory to his nineteenth-century country house in Suffolk (left), and filled it with period wicker furniture, antique earthenware pots and containers overflowing with plants in the opulent Victorian manner, to complement the style of the house. A nineteenth-century urn on the terrace outside the conservatory is topped by a colourful but simple flower arrangement (right). Neoclassical cast-iron urns always lend a touch of authenticity to a period garden, and good modern copies abound in the garden centres. After a few seasons in the garden, the weather will have added rust and patina, making it hard to distinguish between a fake and the real thing.

RIGHT ABOVE *One or two outstanding pieces can make a bold statement in an otherwise plain setting. In the walled garden of a house near Paris, the owner – an antiques dealer – has used a rare tôle* Chinoiserie *pavilion and a pair of curly, wrought-iron garden chairs to enliven the bland surroundings. Although a recent addition, the ensemble blends in so well with the environment that it looks as though it has been there for centuries.*

RIGHT CENTRE *In the courtyard of a mansion in the Hague, an elegant corner has been created using nineteenth-century cast-iron garden chairs and urns, and earlier statuary. The oversized, trellised iron garden bench was made to the owner's own design, but inspired by eighteenth-century examples, as were the box trees clipped into a corkscrew shape. Both the new and the antique garden furniture has been painted in the same bright colour, so it is hard to make out which pieces are original and which are modern.*

RIGHT BELOW *Original features are often best left undisturbed. This old gazebo in the grounds of a Swedish house still has its original finish. The pale blue and cream colour scheme was a very popular one throughout the nineteenth century.*

OPPOSITE *Period architectural features deserve to be emphasized. In Ute Middelhoek's modest garden, the original, round kitchen window and the arch leading to the kitchen garden are surrounded by clusters of ivy. An old garden bench and table and folding chairs provide a cosy corner for relaxation or a meal.*

OVERLEAF LEFT *In a tiny garden, on the cliffs of a village in the south of France, the wrought-iron garden furniture has been painted a dark olive green. Rather than choosing a brand-new parasol, the owners have opted for an antique specimen, whose colour and shape complement the furniture.*

OVERLEAF RIGHT *A secluded, romantic corner has been carved out of a large, formal garden. The arched brick wall contains a shallow niche and fountain, and a reproduction cast-iron 'turn-of-the-century' bench sits among shrubs and flower-filled containers. The sound of splashing water provides an ideal background for a restful afternoon spent reading a book or enjoying tea.*

LEFT *A crumbling Neoclassical stone urn, complete with ancient patina, cracks and obvious restoration, has been placed in the niche of an old garden wall in an Oxfordshire garden. Surrounded by rambling greenery, it is a haunting image of 'period' beauty.*

RIGHT *A garden door, almost completely eaten away by time, still clings miraculously to one of its hinges. If the door had been replaced by a brand-new one, the romance of the entrance to a secret passage leading from the garden to the stables would have been destroyed.*

SOURCE LIST

GREAT BRITAIN

LONDON

Acquisitions Fireplaces Ltd.
24-26 Holmes Road
London NW5 3AB
Tel. (0171) 485 4955
Hand-carved marble fireplaces

Alfie's Antique Market
13 Church Street
London NW8 8DT
Tel. (0171) 723 6066
A large selection of general antiques

J.D. Beardmore & Co. Ltd.
17 Pall Mall
London SW1Y 5LU
Tel. (0171) 637 7041
Reproduction fittings for furniture and for the home in brass and iron

Classic Bindings
61 Cambridge Street
London SW1 4PS
Tel. (0171) 834 5554
Antique books

Joanna Booth Antique Textiles
247 King's Road
London SW3 5EL
Tel. (0171) 352 8998
Antique textiles

Carlton Hobbs
46 Pimlico Road
London SW1 8LP
Tel. (0171) 730 3640
Eighteenth- and nineteenth-century continental furniture

Chalon
The Plaza
535 King's Road
London SW10 0SZ
Tel. (0171) 351 0008
Formal country furniture

The Dining Room Shop
62-64 White Hart Lane
London SW13 0PZ
Tel. (0181) 878 1020
Antiques for the dining room

Andrew Edmunds
44 Lexington Street
London W1R 3LH
Tel. (0171) 437 8594
English and European prints and drawings. Specializing in caricatures and the eighteenth century

The Furniture Cave
533 King's Road
London SW10 0TZ
Tel. (0171) 352 7013
Eighteenth- and nineteenth-century English and continental furniture, objets d'art, paintings, engravings and architectural items

Gallery of Antique Costumes & Textiles
2 Church Street
London NW8 8ED
Tel. (0171) 723 9981
Textiles dating as far back as the seventeenth century

Glass Houses
Barnsbury Street
London N1 1PW
Tel. (0171) 607 6071
Conservatories and orangeries

Gray's Antique Market
1-7 Davies Mews
London W1Y 2LP
Tel. (0171) 629 7034
Objets d'art, jewellery, silver, porcelain and clocks

The London Architectural
Salvage & Supply Company
(LASSCo.)
St Michael's
Mark Street (off Paul Street)
London EC2A 4ER
Tel. (0171) 739 0448
Period floors, panelling, architectural elements and fireplaces

Lunn Antiques
86 New King's Road
London SW6 4LU
Tel. (0171) 736 4638
Antique linens, lace curtains and bedspreads

Paul Mitchell Ltd.
99 New Bond Street
London W1Y 9LF
Tel. (0171) 493 8732
Antique and reproduction frames

Anthony Outred
The Furniture Cave
533 King's Road
London SW10 0TZ
Tel. (0171) 352 8840
Fine eighteenth- and nineteenth-century Neoclassical furniture. Russian and Scandinavian period pieces and sculpture

John Perry's Wallpaper
AVAILABLE FROM:
Cole and Son
Talbot House
17 Church Street
Rickmansworth
Herts WD3 1DE
Tel. (0171) 607 4288

ALSO AVAILABLE FROM:
Chelsea Showroom
Chelsea Design Centre
Lots Road
London SW10 0XE
Tel. (0171) 375 4628
Catalogue supplied on request. Wallpaper hand-printed from wood blocks

Anthony Redmile Ltd.
The Furniture Cave
533 King's Road
London SW10 0TZ
Tel. (0171) 351 3813
Reproduction classical statuary, medallions and wall plaques

Seago
22 Pimlico Road
London SW1 8LJ
Tel. (0171) 730 7502
Garden sculpture and ornaments

Keith Skeel
94-98 Islington High Street
London N1 8EG
Tel. (0171) 226 7012
Antiques and eccentricities, nineteenth-century English and continental furniture, mirrors, chandeliers, sculpture and objets d'art

Through the Looking Glass
563 King's Road
London SW6 2ED
Tel. (0171) 736 7799
Antique mirrors

OUTSIDE LONDON

Antiques and Country Pine
14 East Street
Crewkerne
Somerset TA18 7AG
Tel. (01460) 75623
Country furniture and antique pine

Batheaston Chairmakers
20 Leafield Way Estate
Leafield Industrial Estate
Corsham
Wiltshire SN13 9SW
Tel. (01225) 811295
Antiqued reproduction furniture, especially oak tables and country-style cabinets

Context Weavers
Park Mill, Holcombe Road
Helmshore
Rossendale
Lancashire BB4 4NP
Tel. (01706) 220917
*Reproduction eighteenth-
century country fabrics*

Crowther of Syon Lodge
Syon Lodge
Bush Corner
London Road
Isleworth
Middlesex TW7 5BH
Tel. (0181) 560 7978
*Antiques for the garden and
period architectural elements,
fireplaces, panelling and
ironwork*

Haddonstone
The Forge House
Church Lane
East Haddon
Northampton NN6 8DB
Tel. (01604) 770711
*Classic building materials,
sculpture and garden ornaments*

Hampshire Gardens Craft
Rake Industries
Rake near Petersfield
Hampshire GU31 5DR
Tel. (01730) 895182
*Manufacturers of antiqued
garden ornaments*

Hennessy
42 East Street
Crewkerne
Somerset TA18 7AG
Tel. (01460) 78060
Country furniture

The Old Forge
Huntington Antiques Ltd.
Church Street
Stow-on-the-Wold
Gloucestershire GL54 1BE
Tel. (01451) 830842
Country furniture

Sweerts de Landas
Dunsborough Park
Ripley
Surrey GU23 6AC
Tel. (01483) 225366
*Antique garden ornaments
from the seventeenth,
eighteenth and nineteenth
centuries*

Walcot Reclamation
108 Walcot Street
Bath BE1 5BG
Tel. (01225) 444404
*Architectural salvage and
traditional building antiques*

UNITED STATES

NEW YORK

Danny Alessandro Ltd
Edwin Jackson Inc.
307 East 60th Street
New York, NY 10022
Tel. (212) 421 1928
*Large selection of first-quality
fireplaces, mantels and
accessories*

Architectural Paneling Inc.
979 Third Avenue
New York, NY 10022
Tel. (212) 371 9632
*Fireplaces, mirrors, panelling
and mouldings*

Richard B. Arkway
59 East 54th Street
New York, NY 10022
Tel. (212) 751 8135
*Antique maps, globes, rare books
and atlases*

Beauvais Carpets
201 East 57th Street
New York, NY 10022
Tel. (212) 688 2265
*European and oriental rare
antique and decorative carpets.
European tapestries*

Bernard & S. Dean Levy Inc.
253 East 74th Street
New York, NY 10021
Tel. (212) 288 7569
*French and Russian Empire
antiques. Art Deco and modern
objets d'art*

The Eclectic Collector
1201 Lexington Avenue
(between 81st and 82nd
Streets)
New York, NY 10028
Tel. (212) 249 4277
*Eighteenth- and nineteenth-
century continental antique
furniture and decorative arts*

Laura Fisher
Gallery 84
The Manhattan Art and
Antiques Center
1050 Second Avenue
New York, NY 10022
Tel. (212) 838 2596
*Antique quilts and Americana.
Hooked rugs, paisley and Amish
shawls, antique textiles and
American folk art*

Cora Ginsburg LLC
19 East 74th Street
New York, NY 10021
Tel. (212) 744 1352
*Seventeenth-, eighteenth- and
nineteenth-century antique
textiles, decorations and
needlework. By appointment
only*

P.E. Guerin
23 Jane Street
New York, NY 10014
Tel. (212) 243 5270
Reproduction ironmongery

Michael Hall Fine Arts Inc.
49 East 82nd Street
New York, NY 10028
Tel. (212) 249 5053
*European and American
sculpture in bronze, marble,
terracotta, wood and ivory*

Clinton Howell Antiques
19 East 74th Street
New York, NY 10021
Tel. (212) 517 5879
*Finest seventeenth-,
eighteenth- and twentieth-
century English furniture and
continental objects*

Galleria Hugo
304 East 76th Street
New York, NY 10021
Tel. (212) 288 8444
*Specialists in nineteenth-
century American lighting.
Suppliers to museums and
historic buildings*

Malmaison Antiques
253 East 74th Street
New York, NY 10021
Tel. (212) 288 7569
*Directoire, Empire, French
and Russian furniture and
objets d'art*

The Manhattan Arts and
Antiques Center
1050 Second Avenue at 55th
Street
New York, NY 10022
Tel. (212) 355 4400
*Large antiques emporium.
Period furniture, silver, clocks,
porcelain, chandeliers, rugs, etc.*

Judith and James Milne
506 East 74th Street
2nd Floor
New York, NY 10021
Tel. (212) 472 0107
*Nineteenth- and twentieth-
century American painted
furniture and folk art*

Newel Art Galleries Inc.
425 East 53rd Street
New York, NY 10022
Tel. (212) 758 1970
*Antiques from Renaissance to
French Art Deco, housed in a
six-storey building*

O'Sullivan Antiques
51 East 10th Street
New York, NY 10003
Tel. (212) 260 8985
*Irish Georgian and Victorian
furniture and* objets d'art

Pantry and Hearth
121 East 35th Street
New York, NY 10016
Tel. (212) 532 0535
*Americana and folk art,
painted and high country
furniture from the Pilgrim era
to the late eighteenth century*

Florian Papp
962 Madison Avenue
New York, NY 10021
Tel. (212) 288 6770
*Exquisite eighteenth- and
nineteenth-century English
and continental furniture from
designers such as Thomas
Chippendale and William
Morris*

The Pillowry
132 East 61st Street
New York, NY 10021
Tel. (212) 308 1630
*Tapestry, Aubusson,
needlepoint, Art Deco, Fortuny,
silk, Navajo, kilim, knotted
rug, embroidery pillows made
to order*

Guy Regal Ltd.
223 East 60th Street
New York, NY 10022
Tel. (212) 888 2134
*Italian, French, Swedish and
Russian furniture 1750-1850.
Nineteenth-century
Impressionist paintings*

Ritter Antik
35 East 10th Street
New York, NY 10003
Tel. (212) 673 2213
*Biedermeier, Russian, French,
Austrian, Scandinavian
sixteenth- to eighteenth-
century antiques*

Frederick P. Victoria and Son
Inc.
154 East 55th Street
New York, NY 10022
Tel. (212) 755 2549
*French, English and continental
decorative arts 1700-1830. Period
furniture, clocks and* objets d'art

Woodward and Greenstein
American Antiques
506 East 74th Street (5th floor)
New York, NY 10021
Tel. (212) 988 2906
*Country furnishings, quilts,
architectural elements, pottery and
rag rugs*

S. Wyler Inc.
941 Lexington Avenue
New York, NY 10021
Tel. (212) 879 9848
*Antique English silver, Sheffield
plate, antique porcelain (both
English and Chinese export) and
Georgian glassware*

OUTSIDE NEW YORK

The Buggy Whip Antiques
Southfield, MA 01259
(across from the fire
department)
Tel. (413) 229 3576
*Over 98 antique dealers
specializing in country furniture*

Gerald Murphy Antiques
60 Main Street South
South Woodbury, CT 06798
Tel. (203) 266 4211
*Seventeenth- to nineteenth-
century English and American
furniture, clocks, barometers,
pottery and glass*

Salisbury Antiques Center
46 Library Street (off route 44)
Salisbury, CT 06068
Tel. (860) 435 0424
*Formal English and American
furniture, country furnishings,
paintings and silver*

Salvage One/Chicago
Architectural Salvage Co.
1524 South Sangamon
Chicago, IL 60608
Tel. (312) 733 0098
Architectural artefacts

Hartman Saunders Co.
4340 Bankers Circle
Atlanta, GA 30360
Tel. (404) 449 1561
*Authentic architectural wood
columns*

Joseph Stannard Antiques
Station Place
Norfolk, CA 06058
Tel. (860) 542 5212
*French eighteenth- and
nineteenth-century furniture,
lighting, decorative accessories
and early garden ornaments in
historic Arcanum building*

United House Wrecking
Corporation
Hope Street
Stamford, CT 06906
Tel. (203) 348 5371
*Architectural fragments from
old houses*

FRANCE

PARIS

Michelle Aragon
21 rue Jacob
75006 Paris
Tel. (01) 43 25 87 69
*Furniture, crockery, antique
embroidered linens*

Art Cadre
18 rue de Beaune
75007 Paris
Tel. (01) 47 03 93 56
Antique frames

Auberlet et Laurent
8 boulevard du General Giraud
Saint Maur
Tel. (01) 48 85 95 99
*Decorative plasterwork for the
home – all styles*

Aux Fils du Temps
33 rue de Grenelle
75007 Paris
Tel. (01) 45 48 14 68
*Antique fabrics, 'boutis' from
Provence and a sumptuous choice
of table linens*

Patrice Bellanger
198 boulevard Saint Germain
75007 Paris
Tel. (01) 45 44 19 15
*Seventeenth-, eighteenth- and
nineteenth-century European
sculpture*

Braquenié
111 boulevard Beaumarchais
75003 Paris
Tel. (01) 48 04 30 03
Fabrics

Josy Broutin
8 rue des Francs Bourgeois
75004 Paris
Tel. (01) 42 72 59 80
*Eighteenth- and early
nineteenth-century antiques.
Mirrors, lamps, furniture,
crockery and antique fabrics.
Table and bed linen*

Comoglio
22 rue Jacob
75006 Paris
Tel. (01) 43 54 65 86
*Eighteenth- and nineteenth-
century printed cottons based on
documents of the period*

François Hayem
13 rue du Bac
75007 Paris
Tel. (01) 42 61 25 60
Furniture and objets d'art *from
the seventeenth and eighteenth
centuries*

SOURCE LIST

Dominique Heidenger
Marché Serpette (Marché
aux Puces de Clignancourt)
No 24 Allée 3
93400 Paris
Tel. (01) 45 34 33 85
*Statuary, architectural
elements, salvage and objets
d'art*

Galerie Nicole Altero
21 quai Voltaire
75007 Paris
Tel. (01) 42 61 19 90
*Antique glass, furniture and
objets d'art from the
seventeenth and eighteenth
centuries*

Galerie Golovanoff
21 rue de Beaune
75007 Paris
Tel. (01) 42 61 03 75
*Neoclassical furniture and
objets d'art from northern
Europe and Russia*

Gerard Monluc
7 rue de l'Université
75007 Paris
Tel. (01) 42 96 18 19
*Seventeenth-, eighteenth- and
nineteenth-century furniture
and objets d'art. Also
specializes in earthenware
stoves from the south of France
and northern Europe*

Renotte
61 rue du Faubourg Saint
Antoine
75004 Paris
Tel. (01) 43 43 39 58
*Reproduction fittings for
furniture in all styles*

Christophe Reynal
Marché Paul Bert Stand 421
Allée 7 (Marché aux Puces
de Clignancourt)
93400 Paris
Tel. (01) 40 12 90 77
Antique frames

Girard Sudron
47 rue des Tournelles
75003 Paris
Tel. (01) 44 59 22 20
*Lighting, especially electrical
'candles'*

Le Temps Retrouvé
6 rue Vauvilliers
75001 Paris
Tel. (01) 42 33 66 17
*Antique table linen, bedlinen
and crockery, antique lace and
handkerchiefs*

Galerie Lestranger
Place Saint Jean de Renaud
Saint Rémy de Provence
Tel. (04) 90 92 57 14
*Provençal eighteenth- and
nineteenth-century furniture,
earthenware, drawings and
paintings*

Jean François Hermanovits
4 rue Antoine Gautier
Nice
Tel. (04) 92 04 20 80
*Exceptional furniture and
eighteenth-century objects*

Origines
14 rue d'Epernon Maulette
Houdan
Tel. (01) 30 88 15 15
*Period stone fireplaces, stone
and marble paving, doors and
panelling, architectural
elements and ornaments*

David de Sauzéa
28 rue Ségurane
Nice
Tel. (04) 93 55 88 33
*Unusual furniture and
eighteenth- and nineteenth-
century objets d'art*

Zuber
28 rue Zuber
Rixheim
Tel. (03) 89 44 13 88
*Handprinted wallpapers and
fabrics based on period
documents*

THE NETHERLANDS

Affaire D'Eau
Haarlemmerdijk 148-150
Amsterdam
Tel. (020) 422 0411
*Antique bathroom and kitchens
with accessories*

Anouk Beerents
Prinsengracht 467hs
Amsterdam
Tel. (020) 662 8598
*French and Italian mirrors
from the seventeenth and
eighteenth centuries*

L.J. Mennink
Antiekverkopers
Spiegelgracht 21
Amsterdam
Tel. (020) 627 0933
*Libraries and scientific
instruments*

Van Duyvendijk & Brouwer
Nieuwe Spiegelstraat 46
Amsterdam
Tel. (020) 624 8599
*Antique engravings, etchings
and paintings*

Van Meeuwen Tapijten
P.C. Hooftstraat 101
Amsterdam
Tel. (020) 662 1109
Antique oriental carpets

Pieter van der Aa
Vlietkade 7012
Arkel
Tel. (0183) 56244
*Antique floors from Europe and
America*

Bastings & Van Tuijl
Walstraat 64-66
Oss
Tel. (0412) 623 843
*Chinese porcelain 1682-1722,
Qianlong, Louis XVI and Empire.
Seventeenth- and eighteenth-
century furniture, eighteenth- and
nineteenth-century paintings*

Decoration Empire
Peperstraat 22a
Gouda
Tel. (0182) 583 341
*Engravings from 1500 to 1860,
antique frames and framing*

The English Antique Shop
Graaf de Hompeschstraat 1
Ohé en Laak
Tel. (0475) 551 593
*English oak furniture of the
seventeenth and eighteenth
centuries*

Evers Antieke Bouwmaterialen
De Koumen 58
Hoensbroek
Tel. (045) 522 3333
*Antique fireplaces, doors, floors
and garden ornaments*

Pieter Hoogendijk
Eemnesserweg 91
Baarn
Tel. (035) 542 0459
*Antiques of the Louis XVI period
and hand-painted silk panels*

Luden Antiek & Interieur
Frederikstraat 50-52a
Den Haag
Tel. (070) 361 6607
*Victorian antiques: tables, chairs,
cupboards and armoires*

SOURCE LIST

MCM Antiques &
Eccentricities
Joh. Lenartzstraat 5
Oisterwijk
Tel. (013) 528 8112
*Eighteenth- to twentieth-
century furniture, statuary and
decorative objects*

Ute Middelhoek
Kornewal 4
Buren
Tel. (0344) 572 192
*Eighteenth- and nineteenth-
century folk art, country
furniture, kitchen utensils and
antique linen*

Willem Schermerhorn
Korte Lakenstraat 22
Haarlem
Tel. (023) 531 4770
Antique fireplaces and floors

Van Asperen
Harderwijkerweg 397
Hulshorst
Tel. (0341) 453 217
*Austrian, French and Dutch
antiques from 1700 to 1850*

Ruud van der Neut
Klein Heiligland 43
Haarlem
Tel. (023) 531 7272
*Antique furniture,
earthenware, tiles and Chinese
porcelain*

Johan van der Tak
Oude Groenmarkt 20
Haarlem
Tel. (023) 532 2008
*English Georgian and
seventeenth-, eighteenth- and
nineteenth-century furniture*

GERMANY

BERLIN

Alterna Kontor für antike
Ofen
Pariser Strasse 20
Berlin
Tel. (030) 881 3839
*Cast-iron, enamelled and
earthenware stoves. Also
fireplaces and cast-iron and
antique garden furniture*

Asta von Bethmann-
Hollweg und Volker
Westphal Kunsthandel
Wundtstrasse 52
Berlin
Tel. (030) 321 5502
*Eighteenth- and nineteenth-
century Berlin silver. Sculpture
and Neoclassical furniture*

Buch und Kunstantiquariat
H.H. Koch
Kurfürstendamm 216
Berlin
Tel. (030) 882 6360
*Engravings and books from
1400 to 1950*

Eva Lohmaier
Keithstrasse 19
Berlin
Tel. (030) 213 6862
*Seventeenth-century to
present-day silver from
England and Germany*

Adelbert Stahlmach
Kunsthandel
Eisenacherstrasse 119
Berlin
Tel. (030) 215 2091
*Neoclassical furniture from
Berlin, north Germany and
Russia*

OUTSIDE BERLIN

Antike uhren Peter Heuer
Zur Munte 6
Bremen
Tel. (0421) 211 126
*Eighteenth- and nineteenth-
century clocks and watches*

Antiquitäten Sievert
Tölzerstrasse 129
Gmund
Finsterwald
Tel. (08022) 74877
*Folk art from southern
Germany, country furniture,
ceramics, sculpture*

Konrad O. Bernheimer
Promenadeplatz 13
Munich
Tel. (089) 226 672
*Chinese porcelain, Old Masters
and furniture*

István Csonth
Bamberger Tassenkabinett
Karolinenstrasse 22
Bamberg
Tel. (0951) 53542
*Porcelain cups for tea, coffee and
chocolate, from the eighteenth
and nineteenth centuries*

Kunsthandel Glass
Hans-Luther Allee 21
Essen
Tel. (0201) 774 933
*Sixteenth- to eighteenth-
century Cordoban and embossed
gold leather*

Bernhard ter Hazeborg
Milchstrasse 11
Hamburg
Tel. (040) 410 1016
*Eighteenth- and nineteenth-
century English, north German,
Danish and Swedish furniture*

Karin Jansky
Yorckstrasse 29
Karlsruhe
Tel. (0721) 841 376
*French country furniture,
especially tables*

Keysetlingk & Ladron De
Guevara
Wilhelm-Weitlingstrasse 3
Dresden-Kleinzschachwitz
Tel. (02151) 501 070
*Neoclassical and Biedermeier
furniture*

Benedikt Korth
St Apernstrasse 7
Cologne
Tel. (0221) 257 4838
*Antique wallpaper, decorative
panels, fabrics, panelling and
garden sculpture*

Kunstantiquariat C.G.
Boerner
Kasernenstrasse 13
Düsseldorf
Tel. (0211) 131 805
Drawings and engravings

Kunsthandel Dr Thomas
Schmitz-Avila
Koblenzer Strasse 36 und 55
Bad Breisig
Tel. (02633) 97914
*Furniture from Baroque to
Empire and Biedermeier*

Kunsthandel Schlapke KG
Gabelsbergerstrasse 9
Munich
Tel. (089) 288 617
*Biedermeier furniture and
works of art*

Trax Matthies
Schwarzerweg 5
Hamburg
Tel. (040) 630 7026
*Classical range of building
materials: columns, balustrades,
arches and doorways*

164

Otto Von Mitzlaff Kunsthandel
Römerberg 34
Frankfurt
Tel. (069) 281 482
German furniture of the eighteenth and nineteenth centuries, specializing in furniture by Abraham and David Roentgen

Frank C. Möller
Milchstrasse 10
Hamburg
Tel. (040) 450 35047
Fine arts. Neoclassical furniture. Schinkel garden furniture

Ursula Niedercker
Galerie am Herzogpark
Kufsteinerplatz 5
Munich
Tel. (089) 981 800
Empire and Biedermeier furniture

Urs S. Niederoest
Hohe Bleichen 22
Hamburg
Tel. (040) 344 211
Porcelain from famous German manufacturers (Meissen, K.P.M. Nymphenburg, Ludwigsburg) also furniture, silver and eighteenth- and nineteenth-century Gobelins

Pendulum: Dr Hermann Specht
Maria-Luisenstrasse 5
Hamburg
Tel. (040) 486 214
Eighteenth- and nineteenth-century longcase and regulator clocks

Helga Maria Weber
Eppendorfer Baum
Hamburg
Tel. (040) 478 593
Antique frames from Italy, France, Spain and Germany

Renate Weber
Liszthof 10
Osnabrück
Tel. (0541) 65127
Architectural salvage from England and antique garden furniture

BIBLIOGRAPHY

Robert Becker, *Nancy Lancaster: Her Life, Her World, Her Art*, Alfred A. Knopf, New York, 1996

Françoise de Bonneville, *Rêves de Blanc*, Flammarion, Paris, 1993

Linda Chase and Laura Cerwinske, *In the Romantic Style: Creating Intimacy, Fantasy and Charm in the Contemporary Home*, Thames and Hudson, New York, 1990

Laurence Fleming and Alan Gore, *The English Garden*, Michael Joseph, London, 1979

Julien Green, *Memories of Happy Days*, J.M. Dent and Sons Ltd, London, and Harper Brothers, New York, 1942

Gervase Jackson-Stops (ed.) *The Treasure Houses of Britain: 500 years of Private Patronage and Art Collecting*, Yale University Press, New Haven and London, 1985

Ronald King, *The Quest for Paradise: A History of the World's Gardens*, Whitted Books, Weybridge, and Mayflower Books, New York, 1979

Anne-Marie Nisbet and Victor-André Masséna, *L'Empire à Table*, Editions Adam Biro, Paris, 1988

Stefaan van Raay and Paul Spies (m.m.v Rob van Zoest en Brynn Bruijn, fotografe), *In Het Gevolg Van Willem II & Mary – Huizen & tuinen uit hun tijd*, De Bataafsche Leeuw/D'arts, Amsterdam, 1988

Elke von Radziewsky, *Architektur & Wohnen Selection – Die Besten Antiquitäten-Händler in Deutschland*, 1997

Residence Stijlboek, Residence & Terra, Warnsveld, 1997

Vivian Russell, *Edith Wharton's Italian Gardens*, Frances Lincoln, London, and Bulfinch Press, Boston, 1997

Charles Saumarez-Smith, *Eighteenth Century Decoration: Design and the Domestic Interior in England*, Weidenfeld and Nicolson, London, and Harry N. Abrams, New York, 1993

Peter Thornton, *Authentic Decor: the Domestic Interior 1620-1920*, Weidenfeld and Nicolson, London, and Viking Penguin Inc., New York, 1984

Stella Tillyard, *Aristocrats*, Chatto and Windus, London, and Farrar, Strauss and Giroux, New York, 1994

Michel Tricot and Georges Blanc, *Au Hasard de la Fourchette*, Sang de la Terre/Viva, Paris, 1993

Barbara Ketcham Wheaton, *Savoring the Past: The French Kitchen from 1300 to 1789*, The University of Pennsylvania Press, Philadelphia, and Chatto and Windus, London, 1983

INDEX

Numbers in *italic* refer to
illustration captions

Aalto, Alvar 7
Alessandro II Farnese, Cardinal
    150
armchairs 64, *64*, *67*, 111, *130*
    Colonial *64*, *87*
    Georgian 12, *83*
    Louis XV *130*
    Louis XVI *73*, *115*
    Victorian *83*
    wicker *150*
    wrought-iron *58*
armoire *71*, *129*, *132*

Baldwin, Billy 11
balustrade, wrought-iron *58*
Balzac, Honoré de, 65
Barry, Mme du 138
barometer, Louis XVI *58*
bathing 138–9
bathrooms 136–47
    American country house *144*
    Belanger's 139
    Cinalli's London *143*
    Dutch manor 18, *18*
    French *143*
    Garcia's *143*
    Gauzère's Paris flat *143*
    Haseley Court 139
    Kester's washing area *144*
    Le Mair's farmhouse *35*
    London 'Edwardian' *144*
    Mantovani's *143*
    Méchiche's Directoire *138*
    Metz's *143*
    Parisian *143*
baths, bathtubs, 138, *138*, 139,
    143
batteries de cuisine 97, *98*
bed coverlets, quilted *126*, *129*,
    130, *132*
bed hangings *120*, 121, *126*, *130*
bed linen 121, *126*, *129*, *132*, *143*
bedrooms 118–35
    American country *121*, *129*
    attic *132*
    Curletto's Spanish *124*
    Le Mair's farmhouse *35*
    New England guest 27, *31*
    Normandy *121*
    d'Orgeval's barn *130*
    Parisian *120*, *130*
    Provençal 21, 23, *126*
    south of France house *120*

Suffolk barn *38*
Swiss chalet apartment *129*
Verhoeven's Biedermeier *126*
beds 120, 121, *124*, *126*
    antique military *73*
    day 35, *71*
    draped *à la Polonaise* 18
    four-posters *31*, 120, *121*, *130*
    French metal *132*
    Indian silver *130*
    iron and brass *132*
    lit d'apparat 121, *130*
    Louis XV 120
    Shaker four-poster *31*
    Spanish *124*
    Swiss pine *129*
bedspreads *23*, *121*, *126*, *129*,
    130
Bélanger, François-Joseph 139
benches, *38*, *154*
Bergero, Roberto *82*
Bernini, Pietro 150
Biedermeier style 10, 65, 69, *98*,
    121, *121*, *124*, *126*
birdcages 27, *38*
bookcases 111, *113*, *115*
    Chippendale 44, *47*
Borch, Gerard ter 96
Bretonne, Restif de la *82*
Brighton Pavilion Regency
    kitchen 96–7
Brillat-Savarin, Anthelme *82*
bronzes *115*
Brown, Capability 151
bureau-cabinet, English *64*

cabinets *73*, *87*, *91*
candlesticks *47*, *73*, *91*, 111, *115*,
    143
    cast-iron *31*
    frosted glass *21*
    Georgian 12
    Louis XV *4*
    Louis XVI ormolu *18*
Capodimonte figures *91*
Caprarola, Casino Garden 150
Caracalla, Emperor 138–9
cardboard storage boxes *60*
carpets 9, *64*, *73*
Casdin, Sharon and Jeffrey 27
Castaing, Madeleine 9–10
chairs 9, *88*, *91*
    with cabriolet legs *55*
    carved oak *38*
    'Champagne Chair' 8
    'Dagobert' *143*

Directoire *23*
    dining *87*, *88*
    early American *53*
    eighteenth-century French 23
    eighteenth-century Italian *17*
    garden *154*
    Georgian 27, *27*
    high-backed Colonial *71*, *98*
    Irish *44*
    kitchen *98*, *103*
    ladderback *87*
    Lloyd Loom *71*
    Louis XV *21*, *23*
    Louis XVI *23*, *47*
    Neoclassical *67*, *82*
    nineteenth-century English *58*
    Shaker 27, *31*
    slip-covered 44, *47*
    see also armchairs; sofas
chaises longues *73*, *76*
Chambers, William 151
chandeliers *23*, *53*, *64*, *83*, *124*,
    143
    faux white coral *82*
    ormolu Art Nouveau *83*
    wrought-iron *83*, *88*
Chardin, Jean-Baptiste-Siméon
    21, *82*
Château de la Ferté Saint-Aubin
    9, 13
Château Menou 'period' room
    10
Château of Vaux-le-Vicomte 53
china/porcelain *47*, *58*, *76*, *83*,
    87, *88*, 91, 96
    blue-and-white *4*, *73*, *91*
    creamware 44, *47*, 91
    creil tureens *91*
    dinner services *82*, *91*
Chinoiserie pavilion *154*
Christina, Queen of Sweden
    150
Cinalli, Riccardo *143*
Cinecittà *76*
clocks *111*
    Gustavian bracket *18*
    neo-Renaissance table *115*
    nineteenth-century comtoise
    18
Cocteau, Jean 13
Codman, Ogden 11
Colefax and Fowler 10
Colette 111
colour 8, 10, *18*, 44, *47*, *53*, *53*,
    58, 65, *67*, *82*, *91*, 96, *103*,
    105, *115*, 120, *130*, *154*

conservatory, Skeel's *151*
cooker, Victorian cast-iron *105*
creamware 27, 44, *47*, *91*
crockery *91*, 96, *98*, *103*
Cummings, Rose 11
cupboards *88*, 91, 96, *98*, *103*
    Basque *91*
    corner *21*, *38*, *83*
    Dutch painted *91*
    fitted *98*, *103*
    glass-fronted *91*
Curletto, Hugo *124*

Defoe, Daniel, *Roxana* 65
Delft, Ischa van *87*
Delft tiles 32, *32*, *98*, *105*
Dervieux, Mlle 139
dining rooms 80–93
    American *87*
    Dutch farmhouse *91*
    French chateau *83*
    French farm *83*
    Friesland *88*
    Metz's *88*
    New York apartments *82*, *83*
    Parisian flat *82*, 83
    Robin Hill *47*
    Sjöberg's *87*
    Spitalfields *83*
    Swedish manor house 83
    Victorian 82–3
    village house *87*
Directoire style 10, 11 *17*, *21*, *23*,
    55, *58*, 69, *73*, *82*, *83*, *132*,
    138, 139
'distressed' effects *23*
Draper, Dorothy 11
drawing rooms 62–79
    American country house *71*
    Biedermeier *67*
    Dutch farmhouse *73*
    Jacobean manor *64*
    Massachusetts *71*
    Netherlands *69*
    New England *27*
    New Orleans *64*
    New York apartment *67*
    Paris apartment *73*
    Provençal *21*
    Robin Hill *47*
    Severs's upstairs 12, *76*
    Swiss chalet *71*
    Trulio's Roman *76*
    see also living rooms
duchesse brisée, Provençal *130*
Dutch manor 17–19

earthenware *35, 58, 60, 73*, 96, *96*, 97, *103, 105, 151*
ECART (firm) 9
Eckhart, Jaap *124*
Empire style 65, *69*, 83, *88, 143*
entrance halls 50–61
   eighteenth-century chateau *58*
   French country house *58*
   French Directoire *58*
   Georgian 53
   Hudson Valley house *53*
   Jacobean *55*
   Norman chateau *58*
   Parisian *55*
   Victorian *58*
fabrics 11 *11*, 13, *32, 35*, 64, *64, 73, 96, 120, 121, 126, 130, 132*
Fabritius, Carel 12
firedogs 65, *71*
fireplaces 18, *67*, 69, *76*, 83, *105*
   Adamesque *47*
   Grinling Gibbons 44
   Louis XV-style *120*
   Louis XVI sandstone *69*
   Neoclassical 44
   nineteenth-century plain *69*
fire-screen *124*
floors
   parquet 18, *73*, 83, 138
   parquet-de-Versailles 64
   pine floorboards *103*
   terracotta tiles *69, 83, 88*, 97, *130*
footstool *73*
Fouquet Nicolas, Vicomte 53
Fowler John 10
François I, King of France 82
Frank, Jean-Michel 9
Frederick the Great, King 151
Friedrich Wilhelm II of Prussia 96
furniture *76, 83, 98*, 120
   American country *44*
   anthropomorphic 8
   Biedermeier *69*
   Directoire *21, 73*
   Empire *69*
   garden 23, *151, 154*
   Georgian 11, *12*
   Gustavian *13*
   inflatable, transparent 8
   Knoll 8
   Shaker 27, *27, 31*
   Victorian *32, 73*

Garcia, Jacques *10*, 13, 18, *130, 143*

Gauzère, Jean-Luc *143*
gardens, garden rooms 148–59
   Amsterdam roof terrace *150*
   Dutch country house *150*
   Hague courtyard *154*
   Oxfordshire *158*
   Robin Hill 44
   south of France *154*
   Ute Middelhoek's *154*
gazebos *32*, 150, *154*
George IV, King 96
Georgian style 12, *17, 27, 27*, 44, 53, 83, *83*
Gibbons, Grinling 44
glass/glasses *4, 91, 103*
   cut-crystal Directoire 83
   liqueur *91*
   long-stemmed 'genever' *91*
   mercury *103*
   storage jars *98*
Goethe, Johann Wolfgang von 111
Gray, Eileen 8, 9
Green, Julien 64
Gruffaz, Patrice *82*
guéridon *73*
Gustavian style *4*, 8, 13, 18, *73, 83, 91*, 139
Guyot, Jacques and Catherine *9*, 13

Haseley Court coach house 139
Henri IV, King of France 138
horsehair upholstery *71*
Hogarth, William *82*
Hooch, Pieter de 96, 120
Hörle Herrgard manor *111*
Houdon, Jean Antoine 138
   atelier of 18
Hubert, Serge *55*, 113
Huet, Jean-Baptiste 121
hygiene 138–9

Joseph, James *53, 121, 144*
Josephine, Empress 138
Juhl, Finn 7

Kerr, Robert 111
Kester, Jay Henry *144*
Kew Gardens 151
kilims *64, 115, 130*
kitchen utensils 8, *9*, 18, *35, 38*, 96, *105*
kitchens 83, 94–107
   American country house *97*
   Betje Wolff's *105*
   Brighton Pavilion 96–7
   Château de la Ferté-Saint-
     Aubin *9*

Dutch manor *18*
Dutch town house *98*
Edinburgh flat *105*
French chateau *98*
Le Mair's farmhouse *35*
Leenaer's shop *98*
Marble Palace, Potsdam 96
d'Orgeval's *105*
Suffolk barn 38
Middelhoek's *103*
kitchenware 96, *98*
Kjaerholm, Poul 7

La Fontaine, Jean de, *The Swan and the Cook* 96
La Querrière, Phillippe *121*
La Rochefoucauld, François 53
Lambert, Anna and Günther *58*, 69
Lambert, Anthony *83*
lamps 8, 9, *32*, 76, *113, 115*
   bell-shaped ceiling *55*
   Directoire *23, 73*
   Fortuny 9
   hurricane *58*
   nineteenth-century French *103*
   oil *35, 38, 115, 138*
   reflector wall *27*
Lancaster, Nancy 7, 10, 53, 139
Langhans, architect 96
lanterns *47, 55, 98*
Le Corbusier 8, 64
Le Mair, Cornelis 13
   farmhouse of 11, *32–7*
Le Nôtre, André 150
Leenaers, Karel and Will *58, 98*
libraries and studies 108–17
   French chateau *115*
   French manor house *113*
   Hörle Herrgard study *111*
   Hubert's *113*
   Méchiche's *115*
   Paris apartment *115*
   Thorodoff's *115*
lighting 8, *23*, 44, *129*
lit de repos, French *17*
living rooms
   Dutch *17*
   Le Mair's farmhouse *11, 32, 35*
   Provençal *23*
   see also drawing rooms
lobby, storage *60*
Loudon, J.C., 82–3, 111
Louis XIV, King 53, 150
Louis XV style *4*, 7, *17, 17, 18, 21, 23*, 67, *71, 73, 120, 130*, 139

Louis XVI style 11, 12, *18, 23, 47, 58, 69, 73*, 83, 115, 120
lustre-ware, raspberry *47*

Mallet-Stevens, Robert 9
Mantovani, Stefano *143*
Marble Palace, Potsdam 96
Marie-Antoinette, Queen 10, 151
Marot, Daniel 150
Massé, Jean-Jacques *87*
Maugham, Syrie 11
Méchiche, Frédéric *4, 58, 73, 115, 126, 138*
   south of France home of *12*, 12–13, *21–5, 73*
Mendl, Lady (Elsie de Wolfe) 11
Metz, Maroeska *88, 143*
Middlehoek, Ute *58, 103, 132, 154*
   still life *12*, 13
Mille, Gérard 9
minimalism 9, 12
mirrors *23*, 55, *58, 73, 143*
   Empire giltwood *143*
   Italian giltwood *115*
   Louis XVI *23*
Montaigne, Michel de, 121
Moore, Henry 55
Mourge, M., 8
musical instruments *11, 35*

Naess, Philippa 55, *64*
Napoleon Bonaparte, Emperor, 138
Neoclassical style *4, 18*, 44, *47*, 55, *67*, 76, *82, 115, 138*, 139, *143, 158*
New England home 27–31

obelisks 8, *18, 144*
d'Oberkampf, Monsieur 121
oeil-de-boeuf windows 44, *58, 103*
d'Orgeval, Jean and Dorothée *105, 130*
Oudry, Jean-Baptiste 96

Padberg, Patricia *132*
Paleis Het Loo, Holland 150
panelling 64, 65, *69, 71, 76*, 83, *87, 88*, 139
   Directoire *69*
   Louis XV *17*
   mahogany *144*
   Neoclassical grisaille 65
   pine *44*
   pitch-pine *71, 129*
   tongue-and-groove *87, 103*

INDEX

Panton, Vernon, 'Champagne Chair' 8
Paris: Marché aux Puces 97
Parish, Sister 11
Picasso, Pablo 69
plate rack, Victorian 38
prints and drawings 115, 143
Provençal house, 21–5
Putman, Andrée 8–9

Rabes, Didier 58
Ravesteyn, Sybold van 150
re-edition 9, 91
Regency style 96, 111
Regoût, Petrus, Maastricht, 96
Robin Hill, Connecticut 44–9
Rococo style 73, 87
Rousseau, Jean-Jacques 151
rugs 23, 35, 47, 73

Saladino, John 27, 31, 67, 82, 83
    Robin Hill, home of 4, 44–9
Saladino, Virginia 44, 47
Sanssouci Palace: Chinese pagoda 151
Schiller, Friedrich von, 111
service à la Russe 82
Severs, Dennis, Spitalfields house of 11–12, 12, 76
Sèvres 'biscuit' bust 17
Shaker style 27, 27, 31, 98, 144
shelves 113, 115
    pokerwork 38
silver 44, 83, 87, 91
Sjöberg, Lars 8, 13, 87, 111
    'Gustavian' still life 4

Skeel, Keith, Suffolk house and barn 38–43, 151
sofas 9, 23, 71
    Directoire 73
    eighteenth-century English style 64
    eighteenth-century Italian 73
    Louis XV 18, 73
    Louis XVI 73
    nineteenth-century Italian 73
    Rococo 73
stained-glass windows 32, 35
stairs, staircases 38, 53
    eighteenth-century chateau 58
    French country house 58
    French Directoire 58
    Hudson Valley house 53
    'period' wooden 58
    Provençal 23
    Rabes 'faked' 58
    spiral 44
Starck, Philippe 9
statues and busts 17, 18, 76, 115, 138
    garden 150, 151, 154
Steen, Jan 96
stools, Neoclassical 55, 67
stove, cast-iron Dutch 35, 65
Suffolk barn, Skeel's 38–43

tables 9, 58, 88, 98, 103, 115
    bronze Roman 76
    dining 82, 83, 83, 87
    drop-leaf 83, 87
    eighteenth-century English tilt-top 18

eighteenth-century Provençal writing 23
French Directoire 17
    inlaid marble-top 115
    Italian console 58
    Jacobean 55
    kitchen 38, 98, 103
    Louis XV 67, 71
    Normandy country 83
    perspex 8
    round antique 91
    Swedish Rococo 87
taste 64–5
tazza, nineteenth-century marble 55
tea bin, metal 38
terracotta busts 58, 115, 138
    floor tiles 69, 83, 88, 97, 130
    pots 23, 58, 150
    water cistern 21
Thorodoff, Guy 115
ticking, Friesian Biedermeier 124
Tinterow, Gary 53
Tivoli gardens 150
toile de Jouy 21, 23, 120, 121, 132, 143
tomettes (terracotta tiles) 83
trompe l'oeil 10, 103, 115, 121, 124, 126, 143, 144
Trulio, Andrea 76
tureens 73, 97
    creamware 27
    creil 91
    white china 91
Twombly, Cy 44

urns, garden 151, 154, 158

Vasarely, Victor 8
vases 47, 76, 115, 150
Verhoeven, Arno 124, 126
Vermeer, Johannes 96, 120
Versailles 151
    Escalier des Ambassadeurs 53
    gardens 150
    Grand Couvert 82
Vilmorin, Louise de 13
Vionnet, Madeleine 58
Vliegen, Benoît 71, 129
Von Gontard, architect 96

wall coverings, Liberty 83
wallpaper 23, 64, 88, 113, 121, 139
    Biedermeier 126
    Laura Ashley Réveillon 124
    nineteenth-century grisaille 47, 138
    'Picasso' 7
    toile de Jouy 143
wall-sconces, ormolu 55
Washington, George 60, 87
washstands 138, 139, 143
Wharton, Edith 11
wicker baskets 69, 91, 96, 96, 98, 103, 150
William III, King 150
Wolff, Betje 105
Wood, Ruby Ross 11
Wright, William 151
writing desk 113

AUTHOR'S AND PHOTOGRAPHER'S ACKNOWLEDGMENTS

This book would never have been produced without the stimulating enthusiasm of Caroline Bugler – our editor – and the unwavering support of 'the two Annes' – Fraser and Wilson. We also feel deeply indebted to our publisher Frances Lincoln, who did not hesitate to accept our egocentric proposal. Words cannot adequately thank all who opened their homes, their hearts, their refrigerators and their wine cellars to us, and allowed us to immortalise their interiors and gardens. For permission to reprint copyright material we would like to thank the following: Julien Green from *Memories of Happy Days* (JM Dent and Sons Ltd © Harper Brothers, New York, 1942). Robert Becker from *Nancy Lancaster* (Alfred A. Knopf, New York, 1996, and the Estate of Nancy Lancaster).

PUBLISHERS' ACKNOWLEDGMENTS

The Publishers are grateful to Anne Askwith, Ruth Carim and Maggi McCormick for their assistance in creating the book, and to Helen Baz for the index.

Editor Caroline Bugler
Editorial Assistant Tom Windross
Head of Pictures Anne Fraser
Production Liz Stewart
Art Director Caroline Hillier
Editorial Director Erica Hunningher